Pray One for Another

Pray One for Another

Pray for your Desires

Lennox Anthony Blaides

To order additional copies of this book, contact:
Xlibris Corporation
1-888-795-4274
www.Xlibris.com
Orders@Xlibris.com
63374

CONTENTS

James 5:14

Confess your faults one to another, and pray one for another, that ye may be healed.

The effectual, fervent prayer of a righteous man (person) availeth much.

Mark 11:24-26

Therefore I say unto you, What things soever ye desire, when ye pray, believe that ye receive them, and ye shall have them.

Psalms 37:4

Delight thyself also in the Lord; and he shall give thee the desires of thine heart.

Matthew 6:33

But seek ye first the Kingdom of God, and his righteousness; and all these things shall be added unto you.

Dedication

This book is dedicated to all those who are in need of prayer for one reason or another. There are many who are sick and feel that there is no hope for recovery; some are oppressed; others are depressed; some are confused while others are abused; some feel lost and feel the need of a Savior; some are restless and worried about things beyond their control; and there are some who need encouragement to pray and develop a fruitful relationship with God.

If any of these symptoms or any of a similar nature describes you, then this book is worth reading. There is information in this book than can bring you peace and comfort and help you establish a relationship with God through Jesus Christ. Jesus said in John 14:6, "I am the Way, the Truth and the Life; no one can come to the Father except by me." In John 6:37, he said, "All that the Father giveth me shall come to me; and him that cometh to me I will in no wise cast out."

If you are hurting; feeling depressed, used and abused, rejected and disrespected, there is an answer to your problems inscribed on the pages of this book. Jesus said in Matthew 11:28-30, "Come unto me, all ye that labour and are heavy laden and I will give you rest. Take my yoke upon you, and learn of me; for I am meek and lowly in heart: and ye shall find rest unto your souls. For my yoke is easy, and my burden is light."

Just as two oxen are yoked together to carry the burden, Jesus wants to share the burden with you that you may not become overwhelmed with your sorrows. He wants you to have joy; for the bible says in Nehemiah 8:10, "The joy of the Lord is your strength." In his presence there is fullness of joy; at his right hand there are pleasures for evermore." (Psalms 116:11)

INTRODUCTION

What is Prayer?

WHAT IS PRAYER?

Prayer is the basic fundamental way of communicating with God through his word; either by thought or speech.

Since God is a Spirit (John 4:24), we most often achieve a more stable and fruitful communication with him when we pray in the spirit. This spiritual connection is only made possible through the intervention of the Holy Spirit who helps us in our weaknesses for we do not know what we should pray for as we ought; but the Spirit itself makes intercession for us with groanings which cannot be uttered. And he that searches our hearts knows what is the mind of the Spirit because he makes intercession for the saints according to the will of God (Romans 8:26-27)

It is comforting to know that there are two that intercede for the believer. Jesus intercedes for the believers in heaven while the Holy Spirit interceded for them on earth. The Holy Spirit groans and sighs within the believers as he communes with the Father on behalf of our needs according to the will of God.

Prayer is not just a means of communicating with God but it is also a weapon of our warfare and when executed with the authority given us by Jesus, we can tear down all the strongholds of the enemy. James 5:16 says, "The effectual, fervent prayer of a righteous man (person) availeth much." Proverbs 15:8 and 29 says, "The sacrifice of the wicked is an abomination to the Lord; but the prayer of the upright is his delight." Verse 29 says, "The Lord is far from the wicked, but he heareth the prayer of the righteous."

Do not let prayer be an obligation but rather a lifestyle. God desires to hear from us on a consistent basis that we may build a fruitful relationship with him; full of praise, worship and intimacy.

CHAPTER ONE

The Intimacy of Prayer.

THE INTIMACY OF PRAYER

Most of us know what it is like to have a loved one go on a vacation; and we're left alone till their return.

Some have experienced the sadness that comes with separation through divorce or death.

It is during that time of separation that we feel a greater need to communicate with the other person.

Sometimes it is impossible as in the case of death.

Nevertheless we seem to develop a renewed yearning and desire to become intimate;

And this stems from the loneliness that creeps in as a result of their absence.

So it may be safe to say that it's in this absence that the desire for intimacy is reborn.

Could this be the same when talking about Christianity and prayer; and the love of Jesus?

Bear in mind that Jesus said that he would never leave us or forsake us. Hebrews 13:5.

So if there is a separation from God, we are the ones responsible.

When we depart from him; when we separate ourselves from him who first loved us, we become lonely and desperate for the intimacy that we once shared with him.

Well, this is the type of intimacy that we will be talking about today.

How we may become one with some one; and not just anyone; but how to become one with God through prayer.

Like Jesus said "I and the Father, we are one."

Allow me to read some scriptures to demonstrate how Jesus felt about prayer. What it meant to him on a daily basis.

Mark 1:35

And in the morning, rising up a great while before day, he went out, and departed into a solitary place, and there he prayed.

Intimacy with God through prayer

Luke 5:16
So He himself often withdrew into the wilderness and prayed.

Luke 6:12
Now it came to pass in those days that He went out to the mountain to pray, and continued all night in prayer to God.

Luke 9:28-29
Now it came to pass, about eight days after these sayings that He took Peter, John, and James and went up on the mountain to pray.

29 As He prayed, the appearance of His face was altered, and His robe became white and glistening.

Those four scriptures gives us a panoramic view of the importance that Jesus placed on the urgency and necessity of prayer as a means of communicating with the Father.

Everyone who had the opportunity to spent time with Jesus must have noticed the uniqueness in his daily lifestyle as it pertained to prayer and devotion.

Jesus did not always weep; he did not always become angry. He was nor always hungry or thirsty. He did not always walk to his destination, but one thing for certain it that he always prayed to the Father. He made it his duty to devote himself a various times to pray.

He did not pray the perfunctory prayers like those of the Pharisees who sought praises from men, but he offered up prayers and supplications with strong crying and tears unto him that was able to save him from death and he was heard in that he feared (Hebrews 5:7). He prayed with confidence knowing that that the Father was listening to his prayers (John 11:42). He prayed as someone who had an intimate relationship with God the Father.

The disciples must have observed that special devotion and intimacy and eventually approached him that he would teach them to pray as John the Baptist also taught his disciples to pray; (not as John the Baptist prayed but as Jesus prayed (see Luke 11:1).

They had observed the high priority that he had placed on prayer and came to realize that it was fundamental and the key to an intimate relationship with God.

Prayer

Father
In Jesus' name we come before you;
And we ask for your blessings
We are here today to express our love for Jesus Christ
And to develop an intimacy with you
Through the Holy Spirit;
Teach us the intimacy of prayer
As we study your word.
We ask in Jesus' name
Amen.

In Luke 6:40, Jesus said:
Everyone who is fully trained will be like his teacher.

In Matthew 10:24-25 he taught his disciples a very important lesson.
He said;
"A disciple is not above his teacher, nor a servant above his master.
It is enough for a disciple to be like his teacher,
And a servant to be like his master.
If they have called the master of the house Beelzebub, how much more will they call those of his household!

My friends,
We are of the household of God.
Romans 8:14 says; "For as many as are led by the Spirit of God, they are the sons of God."

Likewise Romans 8:16 declares;

"The Spirit Himself bears witness with our spirit that we are children of God."

And the Holy Spirit is given unto us that he may train us up to be like Christ, the Son of God.

The Holy Spirit will also teach us how to adopt the lifestyle of prayer that is synonymous with Jesus. Jesus knew how to pray for he and the Holy Spirit were also one. The Holy Spirit as we shall see is the engine that takes prayer to the Father.

Romans 8:26-27 declares,

Likewise the Spirit also helps in our weaknesses. For we do not know what we should pray for as we ought, but the Spirit Himself makes intercession for us with groanings which cannot be uttered.

Now He who searches the hearts knows what the mind of the Spirit is, because He makes intercession for the saints according to the will of God.

It is no longer we who prays, but God in us.

Philippians 2:13 says,

For it is God who works in you, both to will and to do for His good pleasure.

My friends, I want you to know that the purpose of this exercise is not simply to encourage you to pray but to help you develop a lifestyle of intimacy communication with God through prayer.

Just as there is intimacy in conversation between husband and wife; there is an intimacy that can be developed with God; and this intimacy is found in prayer.

When we devote ourselves to praying regularly, we are not simply voicing our needs to God; we are actually having both a physical and spiritual meeting with God in the intimacy of prayer.

Just as there is intimacy in the letters written between husband and wife; there is an intimacy to be felt when we meditate on God's Word.

When we meditate on God's word, we are not just reading words on that were printed on paper but we are in fact, having an intimate connection with God through his Word.

So in order to build a strong foundation for a vibrant prayer life, it must be built on the intimacy that we have established with God through Jesus Christ and the Holy Spirit.
Jesus said in John 14:6,

"I am the way, the truth, and the life. No one comes to the Father except through me."

But let me warn you! Discovering the excitement of prayer can be addictive and even contagious.

There is a contagious excitement and an infectious joy when you discover that intimacy that is wrapped up in prayer.

King David had a wonderful intimacy with God and he expressed that intimacy as he penned the Psalms. Reading the Psalms is a good way to learn how to develop an intimacy with God. It is important however that we do not just recite the verses but meditate on them and internalize them as we reach out to God. Allow the message to speak to you as you pour out your soul to the Lord.

Let us begin with Psalm Chapter 1 which is about:

The Way of the Righteous and the Reward of the Ungodly:

The Psalm is listed here for convenience.
Psalm Chapter 1

1 Blessed is the man
Who walks not in the counsel of the ungodly,
Nor stands in the path of sinners,
Nor sits in the seat of the scornful;
2 But his delight is in the law of the LORD,
And in His law he meditates day and night.
3 He shall be like a tree

Planted by the rivers of water,
That brings forth its fruit in its season,
Whose leaf also shall not wither;
And whatever he does shall prosper.

4 The ungodly are not so,
But are like the chaff which the wind drives away.
5 Therefore the ungodly shall not stand in the judgment,
Nor sinners in the congregation of the righteous.

6 For the LORD knows the way of the righteous,
But the way of the ungodly shall perish.

Bear in mind that the goal is to seek after an intimate relationship with God.

This can only be achieved by meeting with him on a regular basis through his word and the assistance of the Holy Spirit.

He will guide your path and show you the way to everlasting intimacy with God.
Psalm 119:105 says,

Your word is a lamp to my feet
And a light to my path.

This corresponds with what Jesus said
In John 8:12 He said,
"I am the Light of the world;
He that follows me shall not walk in darkness,
But shall have the light of life."

In another place, he said,

"Are there not twelve hours in the day? If anyone walks in the day, he does not stumble, because he sees the light of this world.

But if a man walks in the night, he stumbles because there is no light in him." (John 11:9-10)

Beloved,

Jesus is the Light of the world;

He is the Way to the Father;

He is the foundation upon which your prayer-life is built;

He is the one that establishes your intimacy with God through prayer

In John 15:16, he said

"You did not choose Me, but I chose you and appointed you that you should go and bear fruit, and that your fruit should remain, that whatever you ask the Father in My name He may give you."

My time is almost up, but I would like to encourage you to memorize some or all of the verses that we have used today.

Ask the Lord to help you remember his Word John 14:26 Jesus said,

"But the Helper, the Holy Spirit, whom the Father will send in My name, He will teach you all things, and bring to your remembrance all things that I said to you."

Remember:

Don't just memorize a verse. Put it into practice.
James 1:22 says,

Be doers of the word, and not hearers only, deceiving yourselves.

It is not being able to quote a verse from memory that matters; it is God's Word abiding in your spirit that really makes the difference.
John 15:7 Jesus promised,

If you abide in Me, and My words abide in you, you will ask what you desire, and it shall be done for you.

So let me say this; and it's a key to memorization and internalization of God's word;
When you apply a scripture verse consistently and repeatedly to your daily life,
That's when you understand and know the true meaning and effectiveness of that verse!
We pray that God will richly bless you
And enable you to have an intimate relationship with him.
Through his word and through prayer
We pray this in Jesus' name.
Amen.

Send us an Email at
thegateway2heaven@yahoo.com

A Word of Encouragement

In order for us to pray for one another and be effective, we must first have that intimacy with God. So before we indulge in prayers, let us first get to know and understand the one who answers prayers. Let us develop a unique intimacy with the Father of Lights with whom is no variableness, neither shadow of change. Let us develop a love link with the Father because every good gift and every perfect gift comes from him (James 1:17).

Let us first learn to love one another before we can pray for one another. The bible says in 1st John 3:11, "For this is the message that ye heard from the beginning that we should love one another."

1st John 4:20 says, "If a man say, I love God, and hateth his brother, he is a liar; for he that loveth not his brother whom he hath seen, how can he love God whom he hath not seen?"

So as we continue reading this book, I want you to observe the importance that is place on love as the principal ingredient for answered prayer. If you don't have love in your heart, do not pray for anyone because your prayers will not be heard. The bible says in Psalms 66:18, "If I regard iniquity in my heart, the Lord will not hear me."

In Matthew 5:23-24 Jesus said, "If you bring your gift to the altar and there you remember that your brother hath aught against you;
Leave your gift before the altar, and go your way; first be reconciled to your brother, and then come and offer your gift."

That is how important it is for us to forgive each other before we come to God in prayer. Truthful prayer cannot flow out of an unforgiving heart. God knows it and he will not hear it. So how should we pray and what kind of prayers should we offer to God? Chapter two goes into great detail in answering these and other questions.

Notes

CHAPTER TWO

Types of Prayer

PRAYER AGAINST EVIL

What is considered evil to some may be considered good to others and therefore the latter will not pray against their own ideology. The saying that a house divided against itself cannot stand is true, therefore evildoers will not apply a weapon as prayer against their evil deeds.

Who then should pray against evil; and what power does prayer have over evil? Those who seek after God and the well being of mankind should always pray against evil with the power and anointing that comes from God. It is true that behind the murder are the murderers; and behind the evil are the evildoers who are described in the bible as 'serpents and scorpions.' There is a passage of scripture where Jesus alludes to this very thing. In Luke chapter 10, Jesus had commissioned his disciples to go out to the people and deliver the message of the Gospel that 'The Kingdom of God is nigh unto them.' He gave them the power to heal the sick and to cast out demons.

After completing their mission, they returned with joy and spoke of their victory over the evil spirits. Jesus then explained to them saying, "Behold, I give unto you power to tread on serpents and scorpions, and over all the power of the enemy; and nothing shall by any means hurt you." These disciples were given the power to speak against the evil and the evildoers; and they were subjected to the word.

We can preach God's word, evangelize God's word, meditate on God's word, or we can pray God's word; just to mention a few. But how do we define prayer as a weapon against evil? First of all, we did describe prayer as a means of communication with God, and so we must communicate with the Father before we execute the power of prayer against evil. There are two things that I believe to be important in the fight against evil. Number one is to know that you yourself have purged yourself of evil by confessing your sins to God (1 John 1:9-10) and number two is to do what you see the Father doing. Jesus said in John 5:19, "Verily, verily, I say unto you, the Son can do nothing of himself, but what he seeth the Father do; for what things soever he doeth, these also doeth the Son likewise."

So what is the Father's position on evil? The bible says that "every good gift and every perfect gift is from above, and cometh down from the Father of lights, with whom is no variableness, neither shadow of turning. Of his own will begat he us with the word of truth, that we should be a kind of firstfruit of his creatures. Wherefore, my beloved brethren let every man be swift to hear, slow to speak, slow to wrath; for the wrath of man worketh not the righteousness of God." (James 1: 17-20)

So before we open our mouths to speak or to pray, we should always remind ourselves who we are in Christ. We should always commune with the Father through Jesus Christ and the Holy Spirit in order to receive directions for our actions against evil. Our prayers should not reflect vengeance or evil for the evil done against us. 1 Thessalonians 5:15 says, "See that none render evil for evil unto any man; but ever follow that which is good, both among yourselves and to all men." Obviously this statement was made because the believers were probably adopting the old tradition which says, 'an eye for an eye, and a tooth for a tooth.' Some of us may question how can someone pray for evil to befall another? Well, I have personally witnessed prayers of that nature where a believer was praying for harm to come upon another person. When these things happen, our first inclination is to judge that person and put them in the court of public opinion concerning their salvation. Let me ask this question; 'Have you ever said a prayer like that, or have you ever wished for disaster to come upon someone? Think about it as I introduce you to a man that was said to be a man after God's own heart. Let us examine Psalm 35, a prayer of David that is classified as an imprecatory psalm; for he prayed for judgment against his enemies for the wickedness they brought against him.

There are many ways that one can pray against evil, but **Psalm 35** is one of the most imprecatory psalms that goes deep down into the matter and calls for justice to be done. David laid his case before the Lord; not only to show the wickedness of his enemies but also his devotion to the Lord. **I will list this psalm for convenience** and then we will examine some of the verses that form the pattern for an outline of how to pray against evil. Bear in mind that this particular psalm, which is labeled imprecatory is not a prayer of vengeance but an appeal to God to bring an end to injustice and oppression among people. It is also a desire for God to administer justice and reward the wicked with the punishment that they deserve. In his appeal, David does not take vengeance into his own hands, but allows God to make the final decision. He knows that the word of the Lord declares in Leviticus 19:18, "Thou shalt not avenge nor bear any grudge against the children of thy people, but thou shalt love thy neighbour as thyself: I am the Lord." Romans 12:19 says, "Dearly beloved, avenge not yourselves, but rather give place unto wrath: for it is written, 'Vengeance is mine; I will repay, saith the Lord.'

The Psalm is listed here for convenience:

Psalm 35 (King James Version)

¹*Plead my cause, O LORD, with them that strive with me: fight against them that fight against me.*

²*Take hold of shield and buckler, and stand up for mine help.*

³*Draw out also the spear, and stop the way against them that persecute me: say unto my soul, I am thy salvation.*

⁴*Let them be confounded and put to shame that seek after my soul: let them be turned back and brought to confusion that devise my hurt.*

⁵*Let them be as chaff before the wind: and let the angel of the LORD chase them.*

⁶*Let their way be dark and slippery: and let the angel of the LORD persecute them.*

⁷*For without cause have they hid for me their net in a pit, which without cause they have digged for my soul.*

8Let destruction come upon him at unawares; and let his net that he hath hid catch himself: into that very destruction let him fall.

9And my soul shall be joyful in the LORD: it shall rejoice in his salvation.

10All my bones shall say, LORD, who is like unto thee, which deliverest the poor from him that is too strong for him, yea, the poor and the needy from him that spoileth him?

11False witnesses did rise up; they laid to my charge things that I knew not.

12They rewarded me evil for good to the spoiling of my soul.

13But as for me, when they were sick, my clothing was sackcloth: I humbled my soul with fasting; and my prayer returned into mine own bosom.

14I behaved myself as though he had been my friend or brother: I bowed down heavily, as one that mourneth for his mother.

15But in mine adversity they rejoiced, and gathered themselves together: yea, the abjects gathered themselves together against me, and I knew it not; they did tear me, and ceased not:

16With hypocritical mockers in feasts, they gnashed upon me with their teeth.

17Lord, how long wilt thou look on? rescue my soul from their destructions, my darling from the lions.

18I will give thee thanks in the great congregation: I will praise thee among much people.

19Let not them that are mine enemies wrongfully rejoice over me: neither let them wink with the eye that hate me without a cause.

20For they speak not peace: but they devise deceitful matters against them that are quiet in the land.

²¹Yea, they opened their mouth wide against me, and said, Aha, aha, our eye hath seen it.

²²This thou hast seen, O LORD: keep not silence: O Lord, be not far from me.

²³Stir up thyself, and awake to my judgment, even unto my cause, my God and my Lord.

²⁴Judge me, O LORD my God, according to thy righteousness; and let them not rejoice over me.

²⁵Let them not say in their hearts, Ah, so would we have it: let them not say, We have swallowed him up.

²⁶Let them be ashamed and brought to confusion together that rejoice at mine hurt: let them be clothed with shame and dishonour that magnify themselves against me.

²⁷Let them shout for joy, and be glad, that favour my righteous cause: yea, let them say continually, Let the LORD be magnified, which hath pleasure in the prosperity of his servant.

²⁸And my tongue shall speak of thy righteousness and of thy praise all the day long.

. . . . .

Let us look at this psalm, verse by verse and see how we can benefit from the strategies used by David as he offered up his petitions to the Lord.

1Plead my cause, O LORD, with them that strive with me: fight against them that fight against me.

Notice the first thing that David said as he opened his mouth to pray. He appointed the Lord as his advocate to plead his cause, and then he turned the conflict over to him. This is what we have to do when we come before the Lord in prayer; to do battle against the evil ones. We should not take the conflict upon ourselves because these battles are more spiritual than physical, so we must rely on the power of God. 1ˢᵗ Samuel 17:47 says, "And all this assembly shall know that the LORD saveth not with sword and spear: for the battle is the LORD's, and he will give you into our hands." 2ⁿᵈ Chronicles 20:15 says, "Be not afraid nor dismayed by reason of this great multitude; for the battle is not yours, but God's."

There is something that we are required to do when we come to pray against evil and it should become natural to the believers. Since we are constantly in a state of warfare we must adhere to the admonition given in Ephesians 6:10-18 which says,

"10Finally, my brethren, be strong in the Lord, and in the power of his might.

11Put on the whole armour of God that ye may be able to stand against the wiles of the devil.

12For we wrestle not against flesh and blood, but against principalities, against powers, against the rulers of the darkness of this world, against spiritual wickedness in high places.

13Wherefore take unto you the whole armour of God, that ye may be able to withstand in the evil day, and having done all, to stand.

14Stand therefore, having your loins girt about with truth, and having on the breastplate of righteousness;

15And your feet shod with the preparation of the Gospel of peace;

16Above all, taking the shield of faith, wherewith ye shall be able to quench all the fiery darts of the wicked.

17And take the helmet of salvation, and the sword of the Spirit, which is the Word of God:

18Praying always with all prayer and supplication in the Spirit, and watching thereunto with all perseverance and supplication for all saints;"

This should always be our stance; ready and willing to go forward in battle and claiming the victory in Jesus' name.

2Take hold of shield and buckler, and stand up for mine help.

3Draw out also the spear, and stop the way against them that persecute me: say unto my soul, I am thy salvation.

In the midst of the battle, he wants the Lord to assure him that his salvation is of the Lord.

4Let them be confounded and put to shame that seek after my soul: let them be turned back and brought to confusion that devise my hurt.

5Let them be as chaff before the wind: and let the angel of the LORD chase them.

6Let their way be dark and slippery: and let the angel of the LORD persecute them.

As he prayed, he called for the angel of the Lord to be brought in to the conflict.

7For without cause have they hid for me their net in a pit, which without cause they have digged for my soul.

8Let destruction come upon him at unawares; and let his net that he hath hid catch himself: into that very destruction let him fall.

9And my soul shall be joyful in the LORD: it shall rejoice in his salvation.

10All my bones shall say, LORD, who is like unto thee, which deliverest the poor from him that is too strong for him, yea, the poor and the needy from him that spoileth him?

11False witnesses did rise up; they laid to my charge things that I knew not.

12They rewarded me evil for good to the spoiling of my soul.

13But as for me, when they were sick, my clothing was sackcloth: I humbled my soul with fasting; and my prayer returned into mine own bosom.

14I behaved myself as though he had been my friend or brother: I bowed down heavily, as one that mourneth for his mother.

15But in mine adversity they rejoiced, and gathered themselves together: yea, the abjects gathered themselves together against me, and I knew it not; they did tear me, and ceased not:

16With hypocritical mockers in feasts, they gnashed upon me with their teeth.

Here David exposed his character before the Lord as a testimony of his faithfulness to the Word of God; treating others as if they were brothers but receiving injustice in return.

17Lord, how long wilt thou look on? Rescue my soul from their destructions, my darling from the lions.

18I will give thee thanks in the great congregation: I will praise thee among much people.

He promised to praise the Lord for the deliverance he sought of him. In our prayers against evil or for any need we may have, we must always include thanksgiving as a form of gratitude.

19Let not them that are mine enemies wrongfully rejoice over me: neither let them wink with the eye that hate me without a cause.

20For they speak not peace: but they devise deceitful matters against them that are quiet in the land.

21Yea, they opened their mouth wide against me, and said, Aha, aha, our eye hath seen it.

22This thou hast seen, O LORD: keep not silence: O Lord, be not far from me.

Here he pleaded that the Lord be not silent concerning his request, and that he should be close to him. The bible teaches us in James 4:8, "Draw nigh to God and he will draw nigh to you."

23Stir up thyself, and awake to my judgment, even unto my cause, my God and my Lord.

24Judge me, O LORD my God, according to thy righteousness; and let them not rejoice over me.

Verse 24 is crucial in any type of prayer; because one should fee l confident to have God judge them at any time especially in a time of emergency. We never know when a terrible situation could arise leaving us no alternative but to call upon the Lord for assistance; so we should always have a clean heart and confess any sins that we may be aware of. The victory is ours in Jesus Christ; but we must not be hypocritical in our lifestyle for we may appear as those who are crucifying to themselves the Son of God, and putting him to an open shame.

25Let them not say in their hearts, Ah, so would we have it: let them not say, We have swallowed him up.

26Let them be ashamed and brought to confusion together that rejoice at mine hurt: let them be clothed with shame and dishonour that magnify themselves against me.

27Let them shout for joy, and be glad, that favour my righteous cause: yea, let them say continually, Let the LORD be magnified, which hath pleasure in the prosperity of his servant.

28And my tongue shall speak of thy righteousness and of thy praise all the day long.

The prayer ends with four requests; 'Let them not say; let them be ashamed; let them be clothed with shame; and let them shout for joy.'

The first three are against the evil ones, and the last is for the righteous ones. Then he ended the prayer with a promise of thanksgiving and praise to the Lord continually. The bible says in Ephesians 6:18 "we are to pray always with all prayer and supplication for all saints." Sometimes the evil is not against us but against the brethren and this is why the command to pray for one another must be taken seriously. This prayer of David is just one of a number of imprecatory psalms listed in the bible. While Psalm 35 was a plea for judgment, Psalm 69 was a prayer for deliverance; and Psalm 109 a cry for God's help. It is comforting to know that no matter what the situation may be, the Lord is always near to those that love him, and he will fight their battles. We must never forget that we need each other and must continue to intercede for each other in prayer.

Notes

INTERCESSORY PRAYER

Moses (Genesis 32:9-14)

Abraham (Genesis 18:23-32)

The Canaanite woman (Mark 15:21-28)

The Centurion (Matthew 8:5-13)

Elijah and the Widow woman (1 Kings 17)

Prayer of Moses
Exodus 32:9-14

When we pray for each other, we all get prayed for; and in so doing we demonstrate selflessness; but when we pray only for ourselves, we demonstrate self centeredness which is counter productive to the cause of Christianity.

Intercessory prayer is focused outward and not inward; in behalf of someone and not yourself. As a parent, you are more concerned about your children's needs rather than your own; that's the principle behind intercessory prayers. A young Christian, like a baby, tends to pray for his/her desires; but when matured, he/she changes the approach to intercessory prayer as they seek help for others in need.

Intercessory prayers are selfless prayers and are horizontal and vertical in nature; toward others and upward to God. The greatest intercessor we know is Jesus Christ. The bible has a great deal to say about him, which we will discuss in a separate chapter. Hebrews 4:14-15 also Hebrews 7:23-24 says, *"14 Seeing then that we have a great high priest, that is passed into the heavens, Jesus the Son of God, let us hold fast our profession.*

15 For we have not an high priest which cannot be touched with the feeling of our infirmities; but was in all points tempted like as we are, yet without sin."

Hebrews 7:23-24 says, *"And they truly were many priests, because they were not suffered to continue by reason of death:*

24 But this man, because he continueth ever, hath an unchangeable priesthood.

25 Wherefore he is able also to save them to the uttermost that come unto God by him, seeing he ever liveth to make intercession for them."

As for Moses, he was also one of the great intercessors mentioned in the bible; and for the purpose of this study; we will select one of his prayers that we may gain a better understanding of what it means to offer intercessory prayers. Moses was like a parent to the Hebrew children as they journeyed through the wilderness in search of the promise land; and it was his responsibility to provide, protect and instruct them in the way of the Lord. He was continually put to the test, and without the guidance and assistance of the Lord, he would have resulted in failure. There were several instances of rebellion on the part of the Israelites, to the point where the Lord was prepared to annihilate them but Moses intervened with his prayer of intercession. Exodus 32:9-14 describes how Moses pleaded in their behalf. The passage is listed here for convenience:

Exodus 32:9-14 (King James Version)

⁹And the LORD said unto Moses, I have seen this people, and, behold, it is a stiffnecked people:

*¹⁰Now therefore **let me alone,** that my wrath may wax hot against them, and that I may consume them: and I will make of thee a great nation.*

*¹¹And Moses **besought the LORD** his God, and said, LORD, why doth thy wrath wax hot against **thy people, which thou hast brought forth out of the land of Egypt with great power, and with a mighty hand?***

*¹²Wherefore should the Egyptians speak, and say, For mischief did he bring them out, to slay them in the mountains, and to consume them from the face of the earth? **Turn from thy fierce wrath, and repent of this evil against thy people.***

¹³Remember Abraham, Isaac, and Israel, thy servants, to whom thou swarest by thine own self, and saidst unto them, I will multiply your seed as the stars of heaven, and all this land that I have spoken of will I give unto your seed, and they shall inherit it for ever.

¹⁴And the LORD repented of the evil which he thought to do unto his people.

There are several things in this prayer that were significant in producing positive results.
In verse 10, the Lord instructed Moses to leave him alone; but Moses made a conscious decision to stay in communication with the Lord.

(Lesson)

When we come to the Lord in prayer, we should not leave until we get an answer, or experience the peace of God in that petition. Philippians 4:6-7 says, "*⁶Be careful for nothing; but in every thing by prayer and supplication with thanksgiving let your requests be made known unto God.*

⁷And the peace of God, which passeth all understanding, shall keep your hearts and minds through Christ Jesus"

Another example of persistence is found in Genesis 32:24-29, where Jacob wrestled with the angel and refused to let him depart until he was blessed by him. Jacob received the answer to his prayer. He was blessed and also received a name change.

The bible says, "*²⁴ So Jacob was left alone, and a man wrestled with him till daybreak. ²⁵ When the man saw that he could not overpower him, he touched the socket of Jacob's hip so that his hip was wrenched as he wrestled with the man. ²⁶ Then the man said, "Let me go, for it is daybreak."*

But Jacob replied, "I will not let you go unless you bless me."

GE 32:27 The man asked him, "What is your name?"
"Jacob," he answered.

*GE 32:28 Then the man said, "Your name will no longer be Jacob, but **Israel**, because you have struggled with God and with men and have overcome."*

GE 32:29 Jacob said, "Please tell me your name."
But he replied, "Why do you ask my name?" Then he blessed him there.

In verse 11, Moses besought the Lord and reminded him of the good which he did by bringing the people out of Egypt with great power and a mighty hand.

(Lesson)

It is always good to remind the Lord of all the good things he has done for you and others; and to give him thanks and praise, and to bless him for his mercy and kindness.

Psalms 107:1 says, "O give thanks unto the Lord, for he is good; for his mercy endureth forever."

Psalms 103:1-8 says, "Bless the LORD, O my soul: and all that is within me, bless his holy name.

²Bless the LORD, O my soul, and forget not all his benefits:

³Who forgiveth all thine iniquities; who healeth all thy diseases;

⁴Who redeemeth thy life from destruction; who crowneth thee with lovingkindness and tender mercies;

⁵Who satisfieth thy mouth with good things; so that thy youth is renewed like the eagle's.

⁶The LORD executeth righteousness and judgment for all that are oppressed.

⁷He made known his ways unto Moses, his acts unto the children of Israel.

⁸The LORD is merciful and gracious, slow to anger, and plenteous in mercy."

Moses understood the Lord and that's why he was able to plead with him. He feared the Lord but he was not afraid of him.

In verse 12, he reasoned with the Lord and showed him what the enemies would say if he destroyed the Israelites. Then it appeared as if he took command of the situation and urged the Lord to turn from his fierce wrath, and repent of the evil against his people.

(Lesson)

Sometimes we have to take hold of the situation and in the midst of our reverence, or respect, our gratitude, our praise and thanksgiving, we can persuade God to change his mind about a particular situation. When we come to God in the name of Jesus, we are able to do as the bible says in Hebrews 4:16; *"¹⁶Let us therefore come boldly unto the throne of grace, that we may obtain mercy, and find grace to help in time of need."* When we intercede for the needs of others, we are in fact coming before the throne of grace and pleading for mercy for that individual; and the grace that we find is for the purpose of ministering the goodness of God into that person's life. We can then speak words that carry the anointing of the Holy Spirit; and those words will minister grace to that person. The Apostle Paul warns up about the words we speak. Ephesians 4:29 says, *"Let no corrupt communication proceed out of your mouth, but that which is good to the use of edifying, that it may minister grace unto the hearers."*

In verse 13, Moses brought to God's remembrance Abraham, Isaac, and Israel, his servants, and the promise he made to them; to multiply their seed as the stars of heaven; and all the land he promised them and their inheritance for ever. The prayer which Moses brought before the Lord had nothing attached to it that would be of any material or monetary gain to him. This is what true intercessory prayer is all about.

When Moses was finished his petition, he was able to turn the situation around and obtain favor from the Lord. The bible says in verse 14, *"⁴And the LORD repented of the evil which he thought to do unto his people."*

(Lesson)

When you come to the Lord in prayer, in behalf of others, never give up with your plea; never give in to what you might feel, always stick to what you believe. Remind the Lord of his goodness. Do not be afraid to reason with the Lord.

Isaiah 1:18-20 says, "Come now, and let us reason together, saith the LORD: though your sins be as scarlet, they shall be as white as snow; though they be red like crimson, they shall be as wool.

¹⁹If ye be willing and obedient, ye shall eat the good of the land:

²⁰But if ye refuse and rebel, ye shall be devoured with the sword: for the mouth of the LORD hath spoken it".

Now if you think that Moses was able to' drive a hard bargain' let us examine Abraham's prayer for the people of Sodom and Gomorrah.

Notes

Prayer of Abraham
Genesis 18:23-32

Sometimes we think we know everything about a person because we live with that individual, but in reality we may know very little. This is the type of situation that Abraham is faced with when he entered his prayer of intercession.

Sometimes your own children are accused of doing things that you never expect them to do. There are Christians today who are performing acts that may be described as 'nailing Jesus to the cross again and putting him to an open shame.' Let us examine the prayer (plea) of Abraham. The passage is listed here for convenience:

Genesis 18:23-33 (King James Version)

[23] And Abraham drew near, and said, **Wilt thou also destroy the righteous with the wicked?**

[24] **Peradventure there be fifty righteous within the city**: *wilt thou also destroy and not spare the place for the fifty righteous that are therein?*

[25] **That be far from thee to do after this manner, to slay the righteous with the wicked:** *and that the righteous should be as the wicked, that be far from thee: Shall not the Judge of all the earth do right?*

[26] And the LORD said, If I find in Sodom fifty righteous within the city, then I will spare all the place for their sakes.

[27] And Abraham answered and said, Behold now, I have taken upon me to speak unto the LORD, which am but dust and ashes:

[28] Peradventure there shall lack five of the fifty righteous: wilt thou destroy all the city for lack of five? And he said, If I find there forty and five, I will not destroy it.

[29] And he spake unto him yet again, and said, Peradventure there shall be forty found there. And he said, I will not do it for forty's sake.

³⁰And he said unto him, Oh let not the LORD be angry, and I will speak: Peradventure there shall thirty be found there. And he said, I will not do it, if I find thirty there.

³¹And he said, Behold now, I have taken upon me to speak unto the LORD: Peradventure there shall be twenty found there. And he said, I will not destroy it for twenty's sake.

³²And he said, Oh let not the LORD be angry, and I will speak yet but this once: **Peradventure ten shall be found there***. And he said, I will not destroy it for ten's sake.*

³³And the LORD went his way, as soon as he had left communing with Abraham: and Abraham returned unto his place."

Abraham was granted his wish as he interceded in behalf of the people of Sodom and Gomorrah; but was he able to negate the wrath of God against the people? When we examine this prayer, we discover that there were conditions that had to be met. If Abraham had considered that the bible says, "there is none righteous, no, not one; for all have sinned and come short of the glory of God" (Romans 3:10; 23), he would not have set conditions in his prayers.

(Lesson)

If you are the only righteous one in your family, God would spare your household for your sake. But one should never forget that there is none righteous but God alone; and our righteousness comes from the Lord Jesus Christ and his sacrifice on the cross for our sins.

Whenever we come before the Lord in prayer, we must acknowledge our sinfulness and proclaim the righteousness of Christ. We should not determine to know who is righteous because of their good works.

The bible teaches in Ephesians 2:8-10,

"For by grace are ye saved through faith; and that not of yourselves: it is the gift of God:

⁹Not of works, lest any man should boast.

¹⁰For we are his workmanship, created in Christ Jesus unto good works, which God hath before ordained that we should walk in them."

Perhaps, if Abraham had prayed for the salvation of the people without the inclusion of the possibility of finding some righteous, God might have devised a plan to save them all.

A similar situation occurred in the city of Nineveh (Jonah 1:2); but the Lord devised a plan to save the people from destruction. This is another interesting story where the prayer of intercession caused some complications in Jonah's life. This story will be discussed further in chapter 7.

One would think that intercessory prayer should be straightforward; that a person only has to offer a prayer in behalf of another. I feel certain that you would agree that intercessory prayer can take on many forms; from simple desires to spiritual warfare. In the next example of intercessory prayer, demons were involved thus making it a prayer of intercession for the removal of demons.

Notes

Prayer of the Canaanite woman
Matthew 15:21-28

Here is another intercessory prayer offered by a woman who was considered to be 'outside the covenant of Israel' and was therefore classified as 'a dog.' The passage is listed here for convenience:

Matthew 15:21-28 (King James Version)

²¹ Then Jesus went thence, and departed into the coasts of Tyre and Sidon.

²²And, behold, a woman of Canaan came out of the same coasts, and cried unto him, saying, **Have mercy on me, O Lord***, thou son of David; my daughter is grievously vexed with a devil.*

²³ **But he answered her not a word***. And his disciples came and besought him, saying,* **Send her away***; for she crieth after us.*

²⁴But he answered and said, **I am not sent but unto the lost sheep of the house of Israel.**

²⁵ Then came she and worshipped him, saying, Lord, help me.

²⁶But he answered and said, **It is not meet to take the children's bread, and to cast it to dogs.**

²⁷And she said, **Truth, Lord***: yet the dogs eat of the crumbs which fall from their masters' table.*

²⁸ Then Jesus answered and said unto her, **O woman, great is thy faith***: be it unto thee even as thou wilt. And* **her daughter was made whole from that very hour.***"*

What an interesting story! It encapsulates at least seven important ingredients that constitute an effective intercessory prayer. I want to address these seven points and expose the truth that we may all benefit from it. The bible says in John 8:32, "And ye shall know the truth, and the truth shall make you free." The truth does not make you free; it is the knowing of the truth and applying it to your life that makes you free. Smoking cigarettes is dangerous for your health and may even lead to cancer which in turn results in death; but many of us do not know that so we continue to smoke in our ignorance. Others are aware of the danger of smoking but refuse to acknowledge the truth and abandon the habit. So it is when you know the truth and apply it to your life that you are made free. (John 8:31-32)

In verse 22, *the woman approached Jesus and cried out for mercy.*
Notice how she addressed him as Lord, and asked for mercy, not for her daughter but for herself. Hebrews 4:16 teaches that we can come boldly to the throne of grace to seek mercy and find grace to help in time of need. This woman was seeking mercy first then she would find the grace which is the unmerited favor of God upon our lives. This grace is found in Jesus Christ. John 1:14 says, *"And the Word was made flesh and dwelt among us, (and we beheld his glory, the glory as of the only begotten of the Father,) **full of grace and truth.**"* It was only after her plea for mercy that she revealed her daughter's situation saying, "My daughter is grievously vexed with a devil."

(Lesson 1)

Whenever we come before the Lord in prayer, we should first seek his mercy.

In verse 23, *the woman never received an answer, but was told to go away.*

Jesus only listened, while others told her to go away because she was a disturbance, a distraction and a disgrace. When we come to the Lord in prayer, he will first listen to our petitions but may not respond at that moment.

(Lesson 2)

We should never be discouraged if we do not receive an immediate answer from the Lord. When we come to the Lord in prayer, we must remember what we learn in 1st John 5:14-15, *"And this is the confidence that we have in him that, if we ask anything according to his will, he heareth us; And if we know that he hears us, whatsoever we ask, we know that we have the petitions that we desire of him.”*

The woman came on a mission and had no intentions of leaving until she had received the victory. Many people may try to discourage you, by planting seeds of doubt in your mind; but you must reject those thoughts and pursue your goal.

In verse 24, *Jesus announced his mission which would have been devastating to most people.*

He said to the woman, *“I am not sent but unto the lost sheep of the house of Israel.”* It is true that Jesus came to his own people, but his mission was not written 'in stone' for we learn in John 1:11-12, *“He came unto his own, and his own received him not. But as many as received him, to them gave he power to become the sons of God, even to them that believe on his name.”* God loved the world and that's why he sent his Son Jesus Christ; not to condemn the world, but that the world through him might be saved. John 3:16 says, *“For God so loved the world that he gave his only begotten Son, that whosoever believeth in him should not perish but have everlasting life.”* The woman was now aware of Jesus' mission but she felt that her mission was just as important and needed his attention.

(Lesson 3)

When you come to the Lord in prayer, there will always be obstacles in your way but you must use them as opportunities to strengthen your faith. James 1:2-4 says, *“My brethren, count it all joy when ye fall into divers temptations; ³Knowing this, that the trying of your faith worketh patience.*

⁴But let patience have her perfect work, that ye may be perfect and entire, wanting nothing”.

You must never give up or give in to the pressure; press on till you receive the victory.

In verse 25, *She worshipped the Lord, and asked for his help.*
The woman knew how to get the Lord's attention. When she began to worship him, his compassion was aroused and set into motion; but that was not sufficient to prove her cause.

(Lesson 4)

When you come to the Lord in prayer, worship is one of the criteria, but it must be in spirit and in truth. In John 4:24, Jesus said, "God is a Spirit; and they that worship him must worship him in spirit and in truth." We have been given the directive to test the spirits to see if they are of the truth. (1st John 4:1) A desperate person may decide to do anything to save his or her life; but will they give up their lives in desperate pursuit of the Lord or the Gospel? If the answer to that question is 'yes,' then that's a sign of a true believer.

Always worship the Lord first, and then make your request. The Lord is faithful and just; loving and compassionate and he will answer your prayer if it is according to his will. (1ˢᵗ John 5:14-15)

In verse 26, *Jesus reminded the woman about her ethnic background and the disadvantages that were associated with it*.

He said to her, "*It is not meet to take the children's bread, and to cast it to dogs.*" That comment seemed to bear the trademarks of racial inequality; but again it was a test and not a testimony; a comparison but not a condemnation; a name but not a nomination. The truth about the matter is that Jesus loved her and wanted to help her.

(Lesson 5)

When we come before the Lord in prayer, we should not be concerned about our race, the color of our skin, the clothes we wear or the food we eat; we should, according to Romans 12:1-2, "*Present your bodies a living sacrifice, holy, acceptable unto God, which is your reasonable service.*

²And be not conformed to this world: but be ye transformed by the renewing of your mind, that ye may prove what is that good, and acceptable, and perfect, will of God."

Remember that it only takes one word from the Lord to change your life forever and bring you in a perfect relationship with the three persons of the Godhead. In John 14:23, Jesus said, "*If a man love me, he will keep my words: and my Father will love him, and we will come unto him, and make our abode with him.*" In John 14:15-17, Jesus also said, "*If ye love me, keep my commandments.*

16And I will pray the Father, and he shall give you another Comforter, that he may abide with you for ever;

17Even the Spirit of truth; whom the world cannot receive, because it seeth him not, neither knoweth him: but ye know him; for he dwelleth with you, and shall be in you."

In these verses, we recognize a written promise by Jesus that we can be in a perfect relationship with the Father, the Son and the Holy Spirit. The only condition that was set forth was to love him and keep his commandments.

In verse 27, *The woman accepted the truth that she was not a Jew.*
She humbled herself under the mighty hand of God that he may exhalt her in due time. Casting all your cares upon him; for he careth for you." **(1st Peter 5:6-7)**
She was willing to accept whatever the 'elect' would reject. We learn in John 1:11, "He came to his own, and his own received him not. This woman was not one of his own, yet she received him. There is no indication that Jesus gave her power to become a child of God; but what we do know is that she received what she came for.

(Lesson 6)

When we come before the Lord in prayer, we must accept the truth about God's word. In John 14:6 Jesus said, "*I am the Way, the Truth and the Life; no one cometh to the Father except by me."*

1st Timothy 2:4-6 says, "*(God our Saviour) who will have all men to be saved, and to come unto the knowledge of the truth.*

5For there is one God, and one mediator between God and men, the man Christ Jesus;

6Who gave himself a ransom for all, to be testified in due time."

Sometimes the Lord will humble us to prove us; as he did with that woman. Deuteronomy 8:2 says, "*And thou shalt remember all the way which the LORD thy God led thee these forty years in the wilderness, to humble thee, and to prove thee, to know what was in thine heart, whether thou wouldest keep his commandments, or no."*

James 4:6 says, *"God resisteth the proud, but giveth grace to unto the humble."* But we should take the initiative to humble ourselves before the Lord. 2nd Chronicles 7 14 says, *"If my people, which are called by my name, shall humble themselves, and pray, and seek my face, and turn from their wicked ways; then will I hear from heaven, and will forgive their sin, and will heal their land. 15Now mine eyes shall be open, and mine ears attent unto the prayer that is made in this place."*

We should also memorize and internalize these truths and present them before the Lord in prayer as a testimony of your allegiance to his Son Jesus Christ.

Finally in verse 28, *The Lord answered her prayer of intercession and granted her the desires of her heart.*

She received the answer to her prayer because of her faith. Jesus said, *"O woman, great is thy faith: be it unto thee even as thou wilt".*

And her daughter was made whole from that very hour.

Jesus was pleased with the way the woman handled herself in that trying situation. He was impressed with her faith. The bible says in Hebrews 11:6, *"Without faith, it is impossible to please God; for he that cometh to God must believe that he is, and that he is a rewarder of them that diligently seek him."*

(Lesson 7)

When we come before the Lord in prayer, we must come believing and not doubting. In John 20:27, Jesus said to Thomas, *"Reach hither thy finger, and behold my hands; and reach hither thy hand, and thrust it into my side: and be not faithless, but believing."*

This woman may have been at one of Jesus' lectures on the power of faith, and heard him say, "What things soever ye desire, when ye pray, believe that ye receive them, and ye shall have them."(Mark 11:24)

James 1:6-8 says that "we must ask in faith, nothing wavering. For he that wavereth is like a wave of the sea driven with the wind and tossed. Let not that man think that he shall receive anything of the Lord. A double minded man is unstable in all his ways."

It is always good to trust God with all your heart and never to lean on your own understanding. God is good and faithful and is just a cry away. The bible says in Acts 2:21, *"And it shall come to pass, that whosoever shall call on the name of the Lord shall be saved."*

In the next intercessory prayer, we will meet a man whose faith marvelled Jesus.

Notes

Prayer of the Centurion for his dying servant
Matthew 8:5-13

When we intercede in prayer for a family member, one would consider that to be a natural act of love; but when we do the same for people outside our family circle, one takes note of it. In Matthew 5:44 Jesus said, *"But I say unto you, Love your enemies, bless them that curse you, do good to them that hate you, and pray for them which despitefully use you, and persecute you;"*

In the following example of intercessory prayer, we encounter a Centurion, a man who was wealthier than the average person, but disregarded what the critics would say about him as he interceded for his dying servant.
The passage is listed for convenience:

Matthew 8:5-13 (King James Version)

⁵And when Jesus was entered into Capernaum, there came unto him a centurion, beseeching him,

⁶And saying, **Lord, my servant lieth at home sick of the palsy, grievously tormented.**

⁷And Jesus saith unto him, **I will come and heal him.**

⁸The centurion answered and said, Lord, **I am not worthy that thou shouldest come under my roof: but speak the word only, and my servant shall be healed.**

⁹For **I am a man under authority,** *having soldiers under me: and I say to this man, Go, and he goeth; and to another, Come, and he cometh; and to my servant, Do this, and he doeth it.*

*¹⁰***When Jesus heard it, he marvelled,** *and said to them that followed, Verily I say unto you,* **I have not found so great faith, no, not in Israel.**

¹¹And I say unto you, That many shall come from the east and west, and shall sit down with Abraham, and Isaac, and Jacob, in the kingdom of heaven.

*¹²But the children of **the kingdom shall be cast out into outer darkness:** there shall be weeping and gnashing of teeth.*

*¹³And Jesus said unto the centurion, Go thy way; **and as thou hast believed, so be it done unto thee.** And his servant was healed in the selfsame hour.*

As we have done in the previous examples, we will expound on points that are relevant to the development of a successful intercessory prayer life.

In verse 6, *The Centurion made his request known unto Jesus without hesitation.*

No one interrupted him or considered him a disturbance mainly because he was a man of great authority. In spite of the power that was vested upon him, he had to face a higher power in Jesus Christ.

(Lesson 1)

When we come before the Lord in prayer, we must address him as Lord and recognize that he is omnipotent, omniscient, and omnipresent. We must know and believe that he is our Father in heaven and we are his children. Jesus gave us an outline on how to pray and what to pray for. In Luke 11:2-4, he said to his disciples, "*When ye pray, say, Our Father which art in heaven, Hallowed be thy name. Thy kingdom come. Thy will be done, as in heaven, so in earth.*

³Give us day by day our daily bread.

⁴And forgive us our sins; for we also forgive every one that is indebted to us. And lead us not into temptation; but deliver us from evil."

In verse 7, *Jesus responded favorable to the request and agreed to come to the house.*

The Centurion however, did not consider himself worthy that Jesus should come to his house (**Verse 8**), but the people thought otherwise because he had built them a synagogue. (Luke 7:5) So he instructed Jesus to simply say the word and his servant would be healed.

(Lesson 2)

When we come in prayer before the Lord, we must believe that *"he is able to do exceeding abundantly above all that we ask or think, according to the power that worketh in us."(Ephesians 3:20)* We must believe that he can send his word forth to accomplish any task. Isaiah 55:11 says, *"So shall my word be that goeth forth out of my mouth: it shall not return unto me void, but it shall accomplish that which I please, and it shall prosper in the thing whereto I sent it."*

The Centurion explained that he had the authority to command the soldiers and they obeyed him **(verse 9)**; but in that moment of despair, when he needed help from the Lord, he was willing to relinquish his authority and submit to the Lordship of Jesus Christ.

(Lesson 3)

We should always be in a state of submission when we approach the throne of God for ourselves or in behalf of others. We must remember that when we intercede for someone; the first thing that the Lord sees is us; so we ought to come 'clean.' We can only come 'clean' through the blood of Jesus Christ.

In verse 10 *When Jesus heard it, he marvelled.*
There are certain things that can get a reaction from Jesus. For instance:
The sorrow and tears of the ones he loves can make him cry.
John 11:35 says, *"Jesus wept."*

Weariness from a journey can make Jesus thirsty.
John 4:7, Jesus asked a Samaritan woman for a drink of water.

When the temple of God is being defiled, Jesus became angry.
John 2:15, *"He made a scourge of small cords, and drove them out of the temple."*

A person's faith can cause Jesus to marvel as is seen in Matthew 8:10 of this intercessory prayer.

(Lesson 4)

When we come before the Lord in prayer, we must stretch our faith to the limit. Faith is measured by the action that is generated by it. There is a saying, 'Doubt creeps but faith leaps.'
James 1:17, 18 and 26 teaches;

"17Even so faith, if it hath not works, is dead, being alone.

18Yea, a man may say, Thou hast faith, and I have works: shew me thy faith without thy works, and I will shew thee my faith by my works.

26For as the body without the spirit is dead, so faith without works is dead also."

Verse 13 *The man's prayers were answered because of his faith.*
Jesus said, "And *as thou hast believed, so be it done unto thee.*"

(Lesson 5)

Faith along with hope and charity are your greatest weapons for kingdom business and spiritual warfare; so it is important to increase your faith by meditation, prayer and the study of God's word.

Romans 10:17 says, "***Faith*** *comes by hearing, and hearing by the Word of God.*

Ephesians 6:16 says, "*Above all, taking the **shield of faith** wherewith ye shall be able to quench all the fiery darts of the wicked.*"

Ephesians 2:8 says, "*For by grace are ye saved **through faith**; and that not of yourselves; it is the gift of God: not of works; lest any man should boast.*"

Galatians 3:11 says, "*The just shall live by **faith**.*"

Hebrews 11:6 says, "Without ***faith*** *it is impossible to please God.*"

2nd Corinthians 5:7 says, "*We walk by **faith** and not by sight.*"

Ephesians 3:17-19 says, "*That Christ may dwell in your hearts by **faith;** that ye, being rooted and grounded in love,*

[18]May be able to comprehend with all saints what is the breadth, and length, and depth, and height;

[19]And to know the love of Christ, which passeth knowledge, that ye might be filled with all the fulness of God.

1st Timothy 6:12 says, "*Fight the **good fight of faith,** lay hold on eternal life, whereunto thou art also called, and hast professed a good profession before many witnesses.*"

Hebrews 12:2 says, "Looking unto Jesus **the author and finisher of our faith**; who for the joy that was set before him endured the cross, despising the shame, and is set down at the right hand of the throne of God."

James 5:15 says, "*And **the prayer of faith** shall save the sick, and the Lord shall raise him up; and if he have committed sins, they shall be forgiven him.*"

2nd Peter 1:5-7 says, "*And beside this, giving all diligence, **add to your faith virtue**; and to virtue knowledge;*

[6]And to knowledge temperance; and to temperance patience; and to patience godliness;

[7]And to godliness brotherly kindness; and to brotherly kindness charity."

Galatians 5:6 says, "*Faith worketh by love.*"

These are just a few scriptures that pertain to faith and it would do you well to memorize them.

Here are a few points that should be included in your prayer list when interceding for someone:

1. Pray that the person be filled with the Holy Spirit.
2. Pray that the person would develop the mind of Christ through the reading of his word.

3. Pray that the person would develop a lifestyle of praise and worship.
4. Pray that the person would develop a humble spirit.
5. Pray that the person would allow the love of God to be shed abroad in his/her heart by the Holy Spirit which is given to them.
6. Pray that the person would continually seek the anointing of the Holy Spirit in order to win souls to Christ.
7. Pray that the person be in good health even as his/her soul prospers.
8. Pray for the family of that person to be saved, if they are not.
9. Pray that the person would hold himself/herself accountable to a group of believers.
10. Pray that the person would confess their sins on a daily basis.

Notes

Elijah and the Widow woman
1 Kings 17:1-24

1 Kings Chapter 17 gives a magnificent description of the providence of God. There are a number of interesting characters and things; such as the widow woman and the ravens; as well as a number of dramatic incidents which will surely keep you 'glued' to the pages of this book. This chapter must be taken in its entirety in order to fully appreciate the prayers of intercession and the wonderful providence of the Lord. I am quite aware that we are studying the various aspects of intercessory prayer; but wouldn't it be more interesting if I told the story that led up to the need for intercessory prayer; and then expose the various components of that prayer? Any other way, I believe might be boring. The chapter is listed here for convenience.

1 Kings 17 (King James Version)

¹And Elijah the Tishbite, who was of the inhabitants of Gilead, said unto Ahab, As the LORD God of Israel liveth, before whom I stand, there shall not be dew nor rain these years, but according to my word.

²And the word of the LORD came unto him, saying,

³Get thee hence, and turn thee eastward, and hide thyself by the brook Cherith, that is before Jordan.

⁴And it shall be, that thou shalt drink of the brook; and I have commanded the ravens to feed thee there.

⁵So he went and did according unto the word of the LORD: for he went and dwelt by the brook Cherith, that is before Jordan.

⁶And the ravens brought him bread and flesh in the morning, and bread and flesh in the evening; and he drank of the brook.

⁷And it came to pass after a while, that the brook dried up, because there had been no rain in the land.

⁸And the word of the LORD came unto him, saying,

⁹Arise, get thee to Zarephath, which belongeth to Zidon, and dwell there: behold, I have commanded a widow woman there to sustain thee.

¹⁰So he arose and went to Zarephath. And when he came to the gate of the city, behold, the widow woman was there gathering of sticks: and he called to her, and said, Fetch me, I pray thee, a little water in a vessel, that I may drink.

¹¹And as she was going to fetch it, he called to her, and said, Bring me, I pray thee, a morsel of bread in thine hand.

¹²And she said, As the LORD thy God liveth, I have not a cake, but an handful of meal in a barrel, and a little oil in a cruse: and, behold, I am gathering two sticks, that I may go in and dress it for me and my son, that we may eat it, and die.

¹³And Elijah said unto her, Fear not; go and do as thou hast said: but make me thereof a little cake first, and bring it unto me, and after make for thee and for thy son.

¹⁴For thus saith the LORD God of Israel, The barrel of meal shall not waste, neither shall the cruse of oil fail, until the day that the LORD sendeth rain upon the earth.

¹⁵And she went and did according to the saying of Elijah: and she, and he, and her house, did eat many days.

¹⁶And the barrel of meal wasted not, neither did the cruse of oil fail, according to the word of the LORD, which he spake by Elijah.

¹⁷And it came to pass after these things, that the son of the woman, the mistress of the house, fell sick; and his sickness was so sore, that there was no breath left in him.

¹⁸And she said unto Elijah, What have I to do with thee, O thou man of God? art thou come unto me to call my sin to remembrance, and to slay my son?

¹⁹And he said unto her, Give me thy son. And he took him out of her bosom, and carried him up into a loft, where he abode, and laid him upon his own bed.

²⁰And he cried unto the LORD, and said, O LORD my God, hast thou also brought evil upon the widow with whom I sojourn, by slaying her son?

²¹And he stretched himself upon the child three times, and cried unto the LORD, and said, O LORD my God, I pray thee, let this child's soul come into him again.

²²And the LORD heard the voice of Elijah; and the soul of the child came into him again, and he revived.

²³And Elijah took the child, and brought him down out of the chamber into the house, and delivered him unto his mother: and Elijah said, See, thy son liveth.

²⁴And the woman said to Elijah, Now by this I know that thou art a man of God, and that the word of the LORD in thy mouth is truth.

Verse 1, introduces Elijah, the Tishbite as a man of God with a prophetic anointing. He prophesied to a man named Ahab that the dew and the rain would cease for some years according to his prophetic word.

Elijah was prophesying by the anointing that was upon him. It was not the Lord commanding him to speak those words; but rather, he spoke those words by the Spirit of God, and he believed that what he spoke would come to pass. There are times when the Lord would speak through the Prophet, and that is made plain by the statement, "Thus saith the Lord."

The Apostle James made reference to this incident in **James 5:17-18** which says, "Elias was a man subject to like passions as we are, and he prayed earnestly that it might not rain: and it rained not on the earth by the space of three years and six months.

¹⁸And he prayed again, and the heaven gave rain, and the earth brought forth her fruit."

This of course was not an intercessory prayer, but it gave way to the circumstances that caused the Lord to act as if a prayer was offered for a person who was in desperate need of the basic necessities of life; things such as food and water.

Verse 2-4, introduces the Lord who then spoke to the Prophet and gave him a special command; to go and hide himself by the brook Cherith, and he would take care of him there.

We could say that the Lord knew that Elijah's prophecy would come to pass and therefore he was taking the necessary steps protect the Prophet from the suffering that would result from that prophetic word. In such a situation, Elijah had to trust in God's word which says, *"The LORD is my shepherd; I shall not want.*

²He maketh me to lie down in green pastures: he leadeth me beside the still waters.

³He restoreth my soul: he leadeth me in the paths of righteousness for his name's sake.

⁴Yea, though I walk through the valley of the shadow of death, I will fear no evil: for thou art with me; thy rod and thy staff they comfort me.

⁵Thou preparest a table before me in the presence of mine enemies: thou anointest my head with oil; my cup runneth over.

⁶Surely goodness and mercy shall follow me all the days of my life: and I will dwell in the house of the LORD for ever."

The Lord took care of Elijah during those desperate times and he will also take care of us in our desperate times.

God spoke to the ravens and commanded them to provide bread and meat for the Prophet both in the morning and in the evening. The God of the bible is an awesome God with all power in heaven and on earth. He walked on the sea (Mark 6:49); he spoke to the wind and calmed the storm (Mark 4:39); he spoke to the dead and they come alive (John 11:43-44; Mark 5:41-42); he even spoke to a fig tree and commanded it to dry up (Mark 11:12-14 and 11:20-26).

It is somewhat difficult to believe that one could speak to ravens and have them obey; or even to a fig tree and cause it to dry up. This may also sound unbelievable, but sometimes it is easier to speak to a tree or a raven and have them obey than it is for some people to obey God's word. 1st Corinthians 2:14 says, "*But the natural man does not receive the things of the Spirit of God, for they are foolishness to him; nor can he know them, because they are spiritually discerned*".

Elijah had room service both morning and evening. If God desired, he could have commanded the ravens to bless the food; on second thought, perhaps they did.

If God was able to make a donkey talk; (***Numbers 22:27-31*** *And when the donkey saw the Angel of the LORD, she lay down under Balaam; so Balaam's anger was aroused, and he struck the donkey with his staff.*
28 Then the LORD opened the mouth of the donkey, and she said to Balaam, "What have I done to you, that you have struck me these three times?"
29 And Balaam said to the donkey, "Because you have abused me. I wish there were a sword in my hand, for now I would kill you!"
30 So the donkey said to Balaam, "Am I not your donkey on which you have ridden, ever since I became yours, to this day? Was I ever disposed to do this to you?"
And he said, "No."
31 Then the LORD opened Balaam's eyes, and he saw the Angel of the LORD standing in the way with His drawn sword in His hand; and he bowed his head and fell flat on his face")

Or make water to flow from a rock; (***Exodus 17:5-6***, *And the LORD said to Moses, "Go on before the people, and take with you some of the elders of Israel. Also take in your hand your rod with which you struck the river, and go.*
6 Behold, I will stand before you there on the rock in Horeb; and you shall strike the rock, and water will come out of it that the people may drink."
And Moses did so in the sight of the elders of Israel.)

Or the Red Sea to divide in two; (***Exodus 14:21-26***, *Then Moses stretched out his hand over the sea; and the LORD caused the sea to go back by a strong east wind all that night, and made the sea into dry land, and the waters were divided. 22 So the children of Israel went into the midst of the sea on the dry ground, and the waters were a wall to them on their right hand and on their*

left. ²³ And the Egyptians pursued and went after them into the midst of the sea, all Pharaoh's horses, his chariots, and his horsemen.
²⁴ Now it came to pass, in the morning watch, that the LORD looked down upon the army of the Egyptians through the pillar of fire and cloud, and He troubled the army of the Egyptians. ²⁵ And He took off their chariot wheels, so that they drove them with difficulty; and the Egyptians said, "Let us flee from the face of Israel, for the LORD fights for them against the Egyptians."
²⁶ Then the LORD said to Moses, "Stretch out your hand over the sea, that the waters may come back upon the Egyptians, on their chariots, and on their horsemen."); he can certainly make the ravens speak. Elijah drank of the brook which could be compared to the rock that followed the Israelites in the wilderness; from which came water to sustain them. (Exodus 17:5-6)

Verse 7 highlights the tragic news that resulted from the absence of rain.

*⁷And it came to pass after a while, that **the brook dried up, because there had been no rain** in the land.* When Elijah realized that there was no more water, and perceiving that what he did could eventually affect him, he must have prayed. In fact, he did eventually pray for the rain to return. I am sure if the ravens were able to speak, they would have said an intercessory prayer for Elijah and moreover, for each other. The miracle or wonder of the feeding of Elijah was for a season and it ended when the water in the brook dried up. But there is a life lesson to be learned by that experience.

(Life Lesson)

If we have the living water flowing from within us, it will never dry up; and the blessings and miracles of the Lord will be renewed every day. It may be that you are experiencing difficult times at the moment, but there are better days ahead. ***Psalms 30:5*** *says,* "For His anger is but for a moment, his favor is for life. Weeping may endure for a night, but joy comes in the morning." We need to pray always; not only when the times are difficult, but when the days are good and fruitful. We also need to pray not just for ourselves but for others in need. Pray for others to be filled with the Spirit of God; that the river of living water would flow from within them (John 7:37-38); that they would never thirst again (John 4:14).

I feel the urge to pray; not only for you, the reader but for anyone who would read this book in the future.

Father,

I come before you, in the mighty and precious name of Jesus Christ;

And I offer this prayer of intercession in their behalf.

I pray, O God that you would anoint them from the crown of the head to the sole of the feet with an anointing that would carry over into every task, every undertaking and every good deed that would be performed today.

I pray that that they would express the love of Christ to everyone they encounter, whether friend or foe; and that your love would go forth from within their hearts thus causing burdens to be lifted; hearts to be mended and souls to be saved.

I ask this in Jesus' name;

And I give him all the praise and all the glory.

Amen.

Verses 8-10 Another command from the Lord to Elijah instructing him to go to another place.

[8]And the word of the LORD came unto him, saying,

[9]Arise, get thee to Zarephath, which belongeth to Zidon, and dwell there: behold, **I have commanded a widow woman there to sustain thee.**

(Life Lesson)

When one mission is ended, the Lord will send you on another, and that mission may be more difficult than the first; but with the Lord nothing will be impossible. *Philippians 4:13 says, I can do all things through Christ or the anointing which strengtheneth me.*

The transition from one mission to the other was very smooth. Elijah would leave the hospitality of the ravens to be accommodated by a widow woman who would also feed him.

The difference between the hospitality of the ravens and that of the widow woman was profound. The ravens had an unending supply of food, but the widow woman had her last and final meal to share between her son and herself. You might wonder,' what does all this have to do with intercessory prayer?' Anything that has to do with the Lord and your need is a reason for prayer.

Verse 10 says, *So he arose and went to Zarephath. And when he came to the gate of the city, behold, the widow woman was there gathering of sticks: and he called to her, and said,* **Fetch me, I pray thee, a little water in a vessel, that I may drink.**

The widow woman was there just as the Lord commanded. Notice the first thing that Elijah asked of her was a little water. Asking for water is a good way to start a conversation with someone. Even Jesus asked for water in order to initiate a conversation with the Samaritan woman at Jacob's well (John 4:10).

Verses 11-12, And *as she was going to fetch it,* *he called to her, and said,* **Bring me, I pray thee, a morsel of bread** *in thine hand.* *[12]And she said, As the LORD thy God liveth, I have not a cake, but an handful of meal in a barrel, and a little oil in a cruse: and, behold, I am gathering two sticks, that I may go in and dress it for me and my son, that we may eat it, and die.*

The woman was commanded by the Lord to sustain Elijah, but it turn; Elijah would have to sustain her by the Word of the Lord. Jesus said in Mark 4:4, *"Man shall not live by bread alone, but by every word that proceedeth out of the mouth of God."*

The word that comes from God is the word of faith. The bible says in Galatians 3:11, *"The just shall live by faith."*

Verse 13, And *Elijah said unto her,* **Fear not; go and do as thou hast said: but make me thereof a little cake first,** *and bring it unto me,* **and after make for thee and for thy son.**

It was obvious that Elijah was asking the widow woman to do something that was mathematically impossible. She only had enough meal for two;

yet he was telling her to make for three; for him first then for herself and her son. Some things cannot be explained except by saying that they are miracles. For example, how did Jesus feed the 5000 people with five loaves and two fishes (Matthew 14:15-21), or the feeding of the 4000 with seven loaves and a few fishes (Matthew 15:32-38)?

Verses 14-15, *For thus saith the LORD God of Israel, The barrel of meal shall not waste; neither shall the cruse of oil fail, until the day that the LORD sendeth rain upon the earth.*

¹⁵And she went and did according to the saying of Elijah: and she, and he, and her house, did eat many days.

Elijah gave her the instructions, and then he prophesied demonstrating that the command was an utterance from the Lord.

.She obeyed the command of the Lord and the results were positive and fruitful.

Verse 16, *And the barrel of meal wasted not, neither did the cruse of oil fail, according to the word of the LORD, which he spake by Elijah.*

Now this is where tragedy struck and the need for intercessory prayer was urgent.

Verse 17-18 *And it came to pass after these things, that the son of the woman, the mistress of the house, fell sick; and his sickness was so sore, that there was no breath left in him.*

¹⁸And **she said unto Elijah, What have I to do with thee, O thou man of God? art thou come unto me to call my sin to remembrance, and to slay my son?**

She spoke as a woman who was aware of her sinful nature. Her language was similar to that of a man who had an evil spirit and was in the house of God. The story is found in **Mark 1:23-24.** I am deliberately expounding on some of these human characteristics so that you may become familiar with other incidents in the bible. For the moment, they may seem unrelated to the topic of intercessory prayer, but don't be fooled, they will emerge at a later time and prove to be beneficial. **Mark 1:23-24** says, "*And there was in their synagogue a man with an unclean spirit; and he cried out,*

24Saying, Let us alone; what have we to do with thee, thou Jesus of Nazareth? art thou come to destroy us? I know thee who thou art, the Holy One of God." They do seem to have a familiar way of speaking. Could this be normal when a person is convicted by their own conscience about the things they are doing; things that are contrary to the Word of God? In spite of her comments, Elijah turned his gaze from horizontal to vertical and began to intercede in behalf of the woman.

Verse 19 *19And he said unto her, Give me thy son. And he took him out of her bosom, and carried him up into a loft, where he abode, and laid him upon his own bed.*

This was Elijah's intercessory prayer.

As he cried out to the Lord, he questioned whether it was the act of God to slay the child. He did not make an affirmative statement but asked a question. Notice that the prayer was not a perfunctory prayer. It was short, fervent and effectual. He cried out to the Lord and he offered up his petition; believing that the Lord heard his prayer. James 5:16 says, "*Confess your faults one to another, and pray one for another, that ye may be healed. The effectual fervent prayer of a righteous man availeth much*".

Verses 20-24 says, *And he cried unto the LORD,* and said, O LORD my God, *hast thou also brought evil upon the widow with whom I sojourn, by slaying her son?*

21And he stretched himself upon the child three times, and cried unto the LORD, and said, **O LORD my God, I pray thee, let this child's soul come into him again.**

22And **the LORD heard the voice of Elijah**; and the soul of the child came into him again and he revived.

23And Elijah took the child, and brought him down out of the chamber into the house, and delivered him unto his mother: and Elijah said, See, thy son liveth.

(As if to say, I told you so. Compare John 11:40-44, Jesus' conversation with Mary)

24And the woman said to Elijah, Now by this I know that thou art a man of God, and that the word of the LORD in thy mouth is truth.

Mark 16:17-18 is a scripture that can bear witness to what the woman said. Jesus said, "*And these signs shall follow them that believe; In my name shall they cast out devils; they shall speak with new tongues;*

18They shall take up serpents; and if they drink any deadly thing, it shall not hurt them; they shall lay hands on the sick, and they shall recover."

(Lesson)

Intercessory prayer does not have to be lengthy prayers; in fact, you could simply kneel and open your heart before the Lord and allow him to search within. David said in **Psalm 139:23-24,** "*Search me, O God, and know my heart: try me, and know my thoughts:*

24And see if there be any wicked way in me, and lead me in the way everlasting."

The Lord is omniscient and so he knows what is in our hearts. He knows even our secret thoughts. In Matthew 6:32-33, Jesus explained that God the Father knows what we need. This is not limited to clothes, food and shelter; but also to our desires whether they be for ourselves or our friends and family. But the key to obtaining our need is wrapped up in reverence and devotion to God and his righteousness.

There are the times when we desperately need the assistance of the Holy Spirit to help us with our prayers. As a matter of fact, we always need the Holy Spirit to help us in our prayers. **Romans 8:26-27** says, "*Likewise the Spirit also helpeth our infirmities: for we know not what we should pray for as we ought: but the Spirit itself maketh intercession for us with groanings which cannot be uttered.*

27And he that searcheth the hearts knoweth what is the mind of the Spirit, because he maketh intercession for the saints according to the will of God."

Intercessory prayer is a must from a Christian perspective because the bible teaches that we must pray one for another (James 5:14). But in order for our prayers to be heard, there must be forgiveness on the part of the person who is offering the prayers. **Mark 11:25-26** says, *"And when ye stand praying, forgive, if ye have ought against any: that your Father also which is in heaven may forgive you your trespasses.*

[26]But if ye do not forgive, neither will your Father which is in heaven forgive your trespasses."

In the next chapter will discuss the prayer of forgiveness and what it truly means to forgive someone.

Notes

PRAYER FOR FORGIVENESS

Sin and Forgiveness

The Prayer of David

The Prayer of Jesus

The Prayer of Stephen

Sin and Forgiveness

Sin and forgiveness is at the core of the bible and when explored, causes a ripple effect that extends throughout all its pages and culminates in the person of Jesus Christ. There was an incident in the Gospel of Matthew Chapter 9 where the question about the forgiveness of sins was raised. Matthew 9:1-8 says, *"And he (Jesus) entered into a ship, and passed over, and came into his own city.*

²And, behold, they brought to him a man sick of the palsy, lying on a bed: and Jesus seeing their faith said unto the sick of the palsy; Son, be of good cheer; thy sins be forgiven thee.

³And, behold, certain of the scribes said within themselves, This man blasphemeth.

⁴And Jesus knowing their thoughts said, Wherefore think ye evil in your hearts?

⁵For whether is easier, to say, Thy sins be forgiven thee; or to say, Arise, and walk?

⁶But that ye may know that the Son of man hath power on earth to forgive sins, (then saith he to the sick of the palsy,) Arise, take up thy bed, and go unto thine house.

⁷And he arose, and departed to his house.

⁸But when the multitudes saw it, they marvelled, and glorified God, which had given such power unto men." In Luke 5:21, the *scribes and the Pharisees began to reason, saying, "Who is this which speaketh blasphemies? Who can forgive sins, but God alone?"*

While we may have the power to forgive, not sins but trespasses against us; only God can forgive sins. In John 20:22-23, Jesus gave his Disciples the Authority to remit and to retain sins, but in the final analysis, it is Jesus who has to forgive the sins; simply because he is God incarnate. So when we pray for our sins to be forgiven, we are not praying to man but to God alone. When the Apostle John introduced Jesus in the first chapter of the Gospel of John, this is what he said; *"In the beginning was the Word, and the Word was with God, and the Word was God." (John 1:1).*

He concluded in verse 14 by saying, *"And the Word was made flesh, and dwelt among us, (and we beheld his glory, the glory as of the only begotten of the Father,) full of grace and truth."* This statement is a clear indication that Jesus is the voice of God and was manifested for all to see. Hebrews 1:1-3 says, *"God, who at sundry times and in divers manners spake in time past unto the fathers by the prophets,*

²Hath in these last days spoken unto us by his Son, whom he hath appointed heir of all things, by whom also he made the worlds;

³Who being the brightness of his glory, and the express image of his person, and upholding all things by the word of his power, when he had by himself purged our sins, sat down on the right hand of the Majesty on high:"

If that is not enough evidence of the deity of Jesus Christ, allow me to go deeper into the scriptures to unveil even more fundamental truth about the Saviour Jesus Christ. While it is comforting and important to know that our sins can be forgiven; it is equally important to know and acknowledge who is the one that forgives our sins. If there was not a redeemer, we would remain in our sins and separated from God. In John 8:23-24, Jesus said to some of the Jews, *"Ye are from beneath; I am from above: ye are of this world; I am not of this world.*

²⁴I said therefore unto you, that ye shall die in your sins: for if ye believe not that I am he, ye shall die in your sins."

First of all, let it be known that Jesus Christ died for the sins of the world, and was resurrected on the third day to become the resurrected Saviour of the world. John 3:16 says, *"For God so loved the world that He gave his only begotten Son that whosoever believeth in him should not perish, but have everlasting life."* John 19:17-18 says, *"And he bearing his cross went forth into a place called the place of a skull, which is called in the Hebrew Golgotha:*

¹⁸Where they crucified him, and two other with him, on either side one, and Jesus in the midst."

Then came the 'grand finale'; John described the moment in verses 28-30 saying, *"After this, Jesus knowing that all things were now accomplished, that the scripture might be fulfilled, saith, I thirst.*

²⁹Now there was set a vessel full of vinegar: and they filled a spunge with vinegar, and put it upon hyssop, and put it to his mouth.

³⁰When Jesus therefore had received the vinegar, he said, It is finished: and he bowed his head, and gave up the ghost."

There are other references of Jesus' crucifixion and death in other Gospels; for example, Luke 23:33 says, *"And when they were come to the place, which is called Calvary, there they crucified him, and the malefactors, one on the right hand, and the other on the left."* Verse 46 confirms that he died, *"And when Jesus had cried with a loud voice, he said, Father, into thy hands I commend my spirit: and having said thus, he gave up the ghost."*

If those references have not convinced you, here is another; Mark 15:37, *"And Jesus cried with a loud voice and gave up the ghost."* Mark 16:9 declares, *"Now when Jesus was risen early the first day of the week, he appeared first to Mary Magdalene, out of whom he had cast seven devils."* I made reference to a scripture that pertains to Jesus' resurrection because there can be no resurrection if there was no death. If you are still not convinced, I pray that you would have an open mind to allow God to guide you into his truth.

There are many people who have not come to faith in Jesus Christ even though their parents have. Genetic transference does not apply to salvation. God does not have grandchildren. There are no biblical references to indicate that salvation is transferred from one generation to another. It is the gift of God and is given to anyone who would believe in Jesus Christ (John 3:16). That's why he may be referred to as a personal Saviour, hence no one can confess your sins for you, and no one can worship God for you.

Ephesians 2:8-9 says, *"For by grace are ye saved through faith; and that not of yourselves: it is the gift of God:*

⁹Not of works, lest any man should boast."

Romans 10:9-10 says, *"That if thou shalt confess with thy mouth the Lord Jesus, and shalt believe in thine heart that God hath raised him from the dead, thou shalt be saved.*

[10]For with the heart man believeth unto righteousness; and with the mouth confession is made unto salvation."

Titus 3:5-6 says, *"Not by works of righteousness which we have done, but according to his mercy he saved us, by the washing of regeneration, and renewing of the Holy Ghost;*

[6]Which he shed on us abundantly through Jesus Christ our Saviour;"

I hope I have shed a little light on the gift of salvation and how important it is to be forgiven of our sins. Here is a scripture passage that explains the sacrifice in more detail. Hebrews 9:22-28, which says, *"And almost all things are by the law purged with blood; and without shedding of blood is no remission.*

[23]It was therefore necessary that the patterns of things in the heavens should be purified with these; but the heavenly things themselves with better sacrifices than these.

[24]For Christ is not entered into the holy places made with hands, which are the figures of the true; but into heaven itself, now to appear in the presence of God for us:

[25]Nor yet that he should offer himself often, as the high priest entereth into the holy place every year with blood of others;"

[26]For then must he often have suffered since the foundation of the world: but now once in the end of the world hath he appeared to put away sin by the sacrifice of himself.

[27]And as it is appointed unto men once to die, but after this the judgment:

[28]So Christ was once offered to bear the sins of many; and unto them that look for him shall he appear the second time without sin unto salvation."

Forgiveness is the key to a successful relationship with God but the forgiveness of others is a component of that success. Jesus said in Mark 11:24-26, *"Therefore I say unto you, What things soever ye desire, when ye pray, believe that ye receive them, and ye shall have them.*

²⁵And when ye stand praying, forgive, if ye have ought against any: that your Father also which is in heaven may forgive you your trespasses.

²⁶But if ye do not forgive, neither will your Father which is in heaven forgive your trespasses."

Jesus took forgiveness very seriously; and as for its counterpart Unforgiveness, he considered it to be detrimental to one's relationship with God. In Matthew he ministered unto his disciples concerning sin and forgiveness; and this is what he said; *"Moreover if thy brother shall trespass against thee, go and tell him his fault between thee and him alone: if he shall hear thee, thou hast gained thy brother.*

¹⁶But if he will not hear thee, then take with thee one or two more, that in the mouth of two or three witnesses every word may be established.

¹⁷And if he shall neglect to hear them, tell it unto the church: but if he neglect to hear the church, let him be unto thee as an heathen man and a publican." (Matthew 18:15-17).

In that example, Jesus was elaborating on the patience of God who is slow to anger but always will to give a second chance. But one of the disciples, Peter by name, wanted to explore the matter even further by asking a familiar question about forgiveness; 'how many times shall my brother sin against me and I forgive him?' Sometimes we have the same problem with our brethren and we ask ourselves; "How many times must I forgive this brother? His offences against me are becoming a habit and I need to do something about it." Jesus gave the answer to that question by saying, *"I say not unto thee, Until seven times: but, Until seventy times seven."* (Matthew 18:22)

How do you forgive someone?
Why should you forgive?
Should your forgiveness be a secret?
Why should we pray for our forgiveness instead of doing something to acquire it?

We will discuss these questions and provide you with information that will enable you to reach out with a forgiving heart to those who have sinned against you. We will also include some of the prayers that were offered by people seeking forgiveness from God for the awful things they have done.

First let us look at the first question; '**How do you forgive someone?**' When you say to someone, "I forgive you;" you must remember that you are not actually forgiving them but asking God to forgive them. One can therefore say that your act of forgiveness is an intercessory prayer in itself. So the way we forgive is to seek God's intervention in the situation and allow him to search your heart to determine if you are sincere in your desire to forgive. Since the prayer of forgiveness is sometimes intercessory in nature, the person does not have to be present to receive forgiveness. However, because of their lack of knowledge of what has been done on your part, that person may continue to operate in an attitude of guilt, shame and even condemnation.

The most appropriate way to forgive someone is by confrontation, explanation and prayer. James 5:16 says, "*Confess your faults one to another, and pray one for another, that ye may be healed. The effectual fervent prayer of a righteous man availeth much.*"

If confrontation is not possible, then there should be some form of communication by which the both parties could hear each other as the confessions are made. You want to know that the other person has heard and acknowledged your forgiveness. You want to be able to say a prayer together in order to get the Lord involved in the situation. Matthew 18:19-20 Jesus said, "*Again I say unto you, That if two of you shall agree on earth as touching any thing that they shall ask, it shall be done for them of my Father which is in heaven.*

20For where two or three are gathered together in my name, there am I in the midst of them."

(Life Lesson)

God wants to be a part of your everyday life; he wants to share your burdens, your hurts and his joy with you. In Matthew 11:28-30 he said, "*Come unto me, all ye that labour and are heavy laden, and I will give you rest.*

29Take my yoke upon you, and learn of me; for I am meek and lowly in heart: and ye shall find rest unto your souls.

³⁰For my yoke is easy, and my burden is light."

In John 16:24, he said to his disciples, *"Hitherto have ye asked nothing in my name: ask, and ye shall receive, that your joy may be full."*

There are times when we all experience difficulties in forgiving someone who has offended us. In those situations, we need to seek the face of God and ask for **his strength, his wisdom, his grace and his love.**

The strength will come from the Lord. Psalm 73:6 says, *"My flesh and my heart faileth: but God is the strength of my heart, and my portion for ever."*
Most often you may feel justified not to forgive that person; but as a child of God we know that those thoughts are not from the Father of lights; the Lord himself but from the evil one. It is God who loves you and *"gave his Son Jesus Christ to be the propitiation for our sins; and not for our sins only; but also for the sins of the whole world."* (1 John 2:2)
Psalms 27:1 declares, *"The LORD is my light and my salvation; whom shall I fear? the LORD is the strength of my life; of whom shall I be afraid?"*

In those dark moments when forgiveness knocks on your door and you refuse to open it, that's the time you need to ask God for wisdom to answer the call. God has promised to give you wisdom if you ask but you must ask in faith. James 1:5-8 says, *"If any of you lack wisdom, let him ask of God, that giveth to all men liberally, and upbraideth not; and it shall be given him.*

⁶But let him ask in faith, nothing wavering. For he that wavereth is like a wave of the sea driven with the wind and tossed.

⁷For let not that man think that he shall receive any thing of the Lord.

⁸A double minded man is unstable in all his ways."

Always remember to exercise your faith in all situations of life because your life comes from God; and without faith it is impossible to please him (Hebrews 11:6)

As for his grace, we have been given access to the throne room of God where we can go and search for it. Hebrews 4:16 says, *"Let us therefore come boldly unto the throne of grace, that we may obtain mercy, and find grace to help in time of need."*

And finally, we bring to our remembrance how God loved us and gave his only begotten Son to die for our sins that we may have everlasting life; and be in the presence of God. Jeremiah 31:3 says," *The LORD hath appeared of old unto me, saying, Yea, I have loved thee with an everlasting love: therefore with lovingkindness have I drawn thee."*

If God so loved us and forgave us, we ought to forgive others. Colossians 3:12-13 says, *"Put on therefore, as the elect of God, holy and beloved, bowels of mercies, kindness, humbleness of mind, meekness, longsuffering;*

¹³Forbearing one another, and forgiving one another, if any man have a quarrel against any: even as Christ forgave you, so also do ye."

When we call on the Lord for **his strength, his wisdom, his grace and his love** to accomplish the will of God for our lives, he will answer us. God has made a promise to those who love him; and don't be fooled; we only love him because he first loved us. (1 John 4:19) The promise is found in Psalms 91:14-16 which says, *"Because he hath set his love upon me, therefore will I deliver him: I will set him on high, because he hath known my name.*

¹⁵He shall call upon me, and I will answer him: I will be with him in trouble; I will deliver him, and honour him.

¹⁶With long life will I satisfy him, and shew him my salvation."

Every believer can rest assured that God will honour his word and extend all those benefits to them. But even in the midst of this season of blessing and the outpouring of God's love, the enemy is still at work attempting to distract us from our focus on Jesus Christ. A good example is found in Psalms 51:1-13 where David was crying out to the Lord for forgiveness for the dreadful sins.

Notes

Prayer of David

The passage is listed here for convenience:

Psalm 51:1-13 (King James Version)

[1]*Have mercy upon me, O God, according to thy lovingkindness: according unto the multitude of thy tender mercies blot out my transgressions.*

[2]*Wash me throughly from mine iniquity, and cleanse me from my sin.*

[3]*For I acknowledge my transgressions: and my sin is ever before me.*

[4]*Against thee, thee only, have I sinned, and done this evil in thy sight: that thou mightest be justified when thou speakest, and be clear when thou judgest.*

[5]*Behold, I was shapen in iniquity; and in sin did my mother conceive me.*

[6]*Behold, thou desirest truth in the inward parts: and in the hidden part thou shalt make me to know wisdom.*

[7]*Purge me with hyssop, and I shall be clean: wash me, and I shall be whiter than snow.*

[8]*Make me to hear joy and gladness; that the bones which thou hast broken may rejoice.*

[9]*Hide thy face from my sins, and blot out all mine iniquities.*

[10]*Create in me a clean heart, O God; and renew a right spirit within me.*

[11]*Cast me not away from thy presence; and take not thy holy spirit from me.*

[12]*Restore unto me the joy of thy salvation; and uphold me with thy free spirit.*

[13]*Then will I teach transgressors thy ways; and sinners shall be converted unto thee."*

In this prayer of forgiveness, we will notice several prayer points and we will expound on them individually. We should also notice that this particular prayer of forgiveness is not the intercessory type because David is praying to God for his own forgiveness.

David addresses the Lord according to his character and lays his petition before him with a guilty plea; seeking mercy. *"¹Have mercy upon me, O God, according to thy lovingkindness: according unto the multitude of thy tender mercies blot out my transgressions."*

²Wash me throughly from mine iniquity, and cleanse me from my sin.

³For I acknowledge my transgressions: and my sin is ever before me.

He makes four requests of the Lord and expects him to grant them because he is truly sorry for having committed those sins. More importantly, he knows that God is merciful, loving and kind, and will not turn away a sinner that repents. Jesus said in Luke 15:7, *"I say unto you, that likewise joy shall be in heaven over one sinner that repenteth, more than over ninety and nine just persons, which need no repentance."* The key that opens the door to God's heart is **confession.** The bible says in 1 John 1:9, *"If we confess our sins, he is faithful and just to forgive us our sins, and to cleanse us from all unrighteousness."* When we are seeking forgiveness from God, we are, for the most part, seeking his mercy; and for that reason, David begins his prayer with the words, 'Have mercy upon me.' He speaks to God as a friend and reminds him of his wonderful attributes; then he seeks to be cleansed from his sins.

There is no 'good works' that can be done to get God's attention and have him forgive our sins; except the confession of those sins through a broken spirit, a broken and contrite spirit which resulted from the sorrow and grief for having sinned against God. Furthermore, a broken spirit that is not in allegiance with Jesus Christ cannot come before the Father. In fact, no one can come to the Father except by Jesus Christ. Jesus himself said in John 14:6, *"I am the way, the truth, and the life: no man cometh unto the Father, but by me."*

There can be no true repentance from sin without genuine faith in Jesus Christ because he is the one who died for our sins; and to him we must come for forgiveness.

Confession is good for the soul and it is a humbling process that God requires of us that he may forgive and cleanse us from our sins. 1 John 1:9 says, ""*If we confess our sins, he is faithful and just to forgive us our sins, and to cleanse us from all unrighteousness.*" 2nd Chronicles 7:14 says, "*If my people, which are called by my name, shall humble themselves, and pray, and seek my face, and turn from their wicked ways; then will I hear from heaven, and will forgive their sin, and will heal their land.*"

In verse 5, he acknowledges that he was born in sin which coincides with what the bible says in Romans 3:10; 23; "*There is none righteous, no, not one; for all have sinned and come short of the glory of God.*" When we pray for God's forgiveness, we must not hold back any sins that we have committed because God knows them all. Psalms 44:21 says, "*Shall not God search this out? for he knoweth the secrets of the heart*" God knows our secret thoughts (Mark 9:4) so it is unwise and unprofitable to make a partial confession.

David continues his prayer and makes fourteen more petitions that he believes are important in the restoration of his intimacy with the Lord. He is convinced that his sins have separated him from the Lord. The bible says in Romans 8:35-39, " *35Who shall separate us from the love of Christ? shall tribulation, or distress, or persecution, or famine, or nakedness, or peril, or sword?*

36As it is written, For thy sake we are killed all the day long; we are accounted as sheep for the slaughter.

37Nay, in all these things we are more than conquerors through him that loved us.

38For I am persuaded, that neither death, nor life, nor angels, nor principalities, nor powers, nor things present, nor things to come,

39Nor height, nor depth, nor any other creature, shall be able to separate us from the love of God, which is in Christ Jesus our Lord."

When Jesus died on the cross, he paid the full price for our sins. Romans 6:23 says, "*The wages of sin is death;*" therefore sin has no power in separating us from Christ; however, we can choose to separate ourselves from the presence of the Lord and the love of Christ. James 4:8-10 sends a clear message, "*Draw nigh to God, and he will draw nigh to you. Cleanse your hands, ye sinners; and purify your hearts, ye double minded.*

⁹Be afflicted, and mourn, and weep: let your laughter be turned to mourning, and your joy to heaviness.

¹⁰Humble yourselves in the sight of the Lord, and he shall lift you up."

One of the petitions that Davit made cannot be applied to the Christian because of the new Covenant. These are the fourteen additional petitions:

1. **Purge me with hyssop**
2. **Wash me**
3. **Make me to hear joy and gladness**
4. **Hide thy face from my sins**
5. **Blot out all mine iniquities**
6. **Create in me a clean heart**
7. **Renew a right spirit within me**
8. **Cast me not away from thy presence**
9. **Take not thy Holy Spirit from me**
10. **Restore unto me the joy of thy salvation**
11. **Uphold me with thy free Spirit**
12. **Deliver me from bloodguiltiness**
13. **Open thou my lips**
14. **Do good in thy good pleasure unto Zion**

In this prayer of forgiveness, David took the time to intercede for Zion; and that must have pleased the Lord. God is pleased when we turn our eyes away from our problems and begin to intercede for others.

In petition number nine, David pleads with the Lord that **he should not take his Holy Spirit from him.** Under the old Covenant, that prayer was acceptable; but under the new Covenant the believer receives the Holy Spirit who will be with them forever. John 14:16-17, Jesus said, *"And I will pray the Father, and he shall give you another Comforter, that he may abide with you for ever;*

[17]Even the Spirit of truth; whom the world cannot receive, because it seeth him not, neither knoweth him: but ye know him; for he dwelleth with you, and shall be in you."

There are four points in this prayer that I consider very outstanding, namely:

To ask for mercy

To make a total confession

To intercede for others

To give thanks and praise

If we follow these guidelines, and "believe that God hears us, we will receive the petitions that we ask of the Lord (1 John 5:14-15).

Notes

The Prayer of Jesus

Luke 23:34

When Jesus was crucified on the cross, he prayed that the Father would forgive those who had crucified him; he also took the initiative to promise forgiveness to one of the malefactors who was crucified alongside him. The account is found in the gospel of Luke Chapter 23, verses 33-43. The passage is listed here for convenience:

"Father, forgive them; for they know not what they do".

Luke 23:33-43 (King James Version)

[33]And when they were come to the place, which is called Calvary, there they crucified him, and the malefactors, one on the right hand, and the other on the left.

*[34]Then said Jesus, **Father, forgive them; for they know not what they do**. And they parted his raiment, and cast lots.*

[35]And the people stood beholding. And the rulers also with them derided him, saying, He saved others; let him save himself, if he be Christ, the chosen of God.

[36]And the soldiers also mocked him, coming to him, and offering him vinegar,

[37]And saying, If thou be the king of the Jews, save thyself.

[38]And a superscription also was written over him in letters of Greek, and Latin, and Hebrew, THIS IS THE KING OF THE JEWS.

[39]And one of the malefactors which were hanged railed on him, saying, If thou be Christ, save thyself and us.

[40]But the other answering rebuked him, saying, Dost not thou fear God, seeing thou art in the same condemnation?

[41]And we indeed justly; for we receive the due reward of our deeds: but this man hath done nothing amiss.

[42]And he said unto Jesus, Lord, remember me when thou comest into thy kingdom.

[43]And Jesus said unto him, Verily I say unto thee, Today shalt thou be with me in paradise."

This may be the shortest prayer for forgiveness that is listed in the bible; along with the prayer of Stephen; but undoubtedly the most fervent and effectual of all prayers because it was offered by Jesus. It was an intercessory prayer because Jesus could not have forgiven the thief on the cross because he was made to be sin and hence could not forgive sins. The forgiveness was left up to God the Father.

Jesus, as the bible teaches us, was without sin and that's why he was *'the sacrificial lamb of God that taketh away the sin of the world'* (John 1:29); but on the day of his crucifixion, he bore the sin of the world and was suffering the consequences. The bible says in 2 Corinthians 5:21, *"For he (God) hath made him to be sin for us, who knew no sin; that we might be made the righteousness of God in him."*

When I say that Jesus could not have forgiven the thief on the cross, I was not referring to it as impossibility because with God all things are possible. But all things must be done in order and without confusion especially in the kingdom of God. When Jesus hung on the cross and the law of imputation was enacted, he became the sin bearer of the world and thus separated from God. That is what sin was able to accomplish in this world. In Matthew 27:46, Jesus cried, *"My God, my God, why hast thou forsaken me?"* Jesus died as a forsaken man; that we might not be forsaken. He surrendered all his power and glory and suffered a shameful death; a death that was considered to be a curse that we might live free from the power and wages of sin. Galatians 3:13 says, *"Christ hath redeemed us from the curse of the law, being made a curse for us: for it is written, Cursed is every one that hangeth on a tree."*

On the other hand, if Jesus was not resurrected, we would all be still in our sins and we would also die in our sins. If the death of Jesus was designed for the forgiveness and reunification of all mankind with the Father, it would not seem fitting for him to forgive sin while he was dying on the cross. It would be more logical to have the plan of salvation executed and brought to its full completion on the day of resurrection. Then all the world would know that the death of Jesus on the cross was made as a substitution for our sins and we can be forgiven by the same Jesus who said in Matthew 9:6, *"But that ye may know that the Son of man hath power on earth to forgive sins;"*

The bible makes it quite clear that *"If we confess our sins, he is faithful and just to forgive us our sins, and to cleanse us from all unrighteousness."* The prayer of Jesus, petitioning the Father to forgive all who shared in making his crucifixion a reality was also meant for us today because the bible says in Romans 3:10 and 23, *"There is none righteous, no, not one; For all have sinned and come short of the glory of God."* We are all sinners and need the forgiveness of Jesus Christ, Our Lord and Saviour. Just as Jesus, with his last breath, asked the Father to forgive us; so must we with our first breath, when we offer our prayers, ask Jesus to forgive us.

Forgiveness is a choice that we make which Jesus insisted that we perform as often as possible. In Luke 6:37, he said, *"Forgive and ye shall be forgiven."* In Luke 17:4, he said, *"If your brother trespass against you seven times in a day, and come to you seven times and asked forgiveness; you must forgive him."*

Ephesians 4:32 says, "*And be ye kind one to another, tenderhearted, forgiving one another; even as God for Christ's sake hath forgiven you.*" Colossians 3:12-13 reiterates the same message; "*Put on therefore, as the elect of God, holy and beloved, bowels of mercies, kindness, humbleness of mind, meekness, longsuffering;*

Forbearing one another, and forgiving one another, if any man have a quarrel against any: even as Christ forgave you, so also do ye."

Jesus paid the price for sin, and he prayed for the unity of the church which we will discuss in another chapter; but because of this new covenant (Matthew 26:26-28), and the dispensation of grace through Jesus Christ (John 1:16-17), we have this wonderful promise in Philippians 1:6 which says, " . . . . *He which hath begun a good work in you will perform it until the day of Jesus Christ.*" Now that we have the assurance that God will complete the work of salvation in our lives, we can feel confident that nothing will be able to separate us from the love of God which is in Christ Jesus our Lord (Romans 8:38-39).

There is another splendid example of forgiveness by a man named Stephen who petitioned the Lord even while he was being stoned to death. There is something quite remarkable about this incident that I feel compelled to share it with you.

The Prayer of Stephen

(Acts 7:60)

It is common practice to stand when the Pastor is saying the opening prayer and we think nothing of it; but what would you say if Jesus were to stand up when you were saying your prayers? Now that's something unusual but not altogether unheard of. In this prayer for forgiveness offered up by Stephen is the only prayer recorded in the Gospel where Jesus was actually standing instead of sitting at the right hand of God. (Acts 7:55-56

For example, Mark concluded his gospel and attributed one verse to the ascension of Jesus Christ: Mark 16:19 which says "*So then after the Lord had spoken unto them, he was received up into heaven, and **sat on the right hand of God.***"

The Apostle Paul confirmed that statement by saying to the Colossians. (Colossians 3:1) *"If ye then be risen with Christ, seek those things which are above where Christ **sitteth on the right hand of God.**"*
Hebrews 1:3 says, *"(The Son, Jesus) Who being the brightness of (God's) his glory, and the express image of his person, and upholding all things by the word of his power, when he had by himself purged our sins, **sat down on the right hand of the Majesty on high:***
Hebrews 10:12 makes this statement about Jesus; *"But this man, after he had offered one sacrifice for sins for ever, sat down on the right hand of God;"*

But what I learned about being at the right hand of God, whether sitting or standing is expressed in Psalms 16:11 which says, *"Thou wilt show me the path of life: in thy presence is fulness of joy; at thy right hand there are pleasures for evermore."*
Stephen was a man filled with the Holy Ghost and was indeed filled with joy. His prayer for forgiveness was occasioned by circumstances similar to those of Jesus. He was stoned to death for exposing some Jewish leaders for their hypocrisy and stiffnecked attitude toward the Holy Ghost and Jesus Christ (Acts 7:51-52).

Stephen's prayer was not imprecatory in any way because he was seeking forgiveness for those who were persecuting him. Matthew 5:44 says, *"Love your enemies, bless them that curse you, do good to them that hate you, and pray for them which despitefully use you, and persecute you;"*
In his agony, Stephen looked up to heaven as if to say, "Where are you, Lord?" The Lord Jesus did appear to Stephen to comfort him in his darkest moment; and he will be there to comfort us in our darkest moments. Stephen then shouted with excitement, in spite of all the pain and suffering; *"Behold, I see the heavens opened, and the Son of man standing on the right hand of God."* His prayer was quick and short because he knew that very soon he would give up the ghost on account of the stoning. He prayed, *"Lord, lay not this sin to their charge."* And when he had said the prayer, he fell asleep.

There are many people on their dying bed who may not have the opportunity to offer a prayer of forgiveness for themselves or someone else. Most of us indulge in procrastination and then become the victims of our own carnal nature. We must let the world know that there is hope for a better life and that hope is in the Lord Jesus Christ. A simple prayer seeking forgiveness and accepting Jesus Christ as Lord and Saviour will change their lives forever; and like Stephen, when they fall asleep, they can rest assured that they will be in the presence of the Lord for all eternity.

(Prayer)

Father,
I come before you, in the name of Jesus Christ;
And I acknowledge that I have sinned against you.
I am asking you to forgive me and cleanse me from all unrighteousness.
Set me free, O Lord from the sin of _____;
Fill me with your Holy Spirit that I may have the power to withstand the wiles of the devil;
That I may be able to praise and worship you in spirit and in truth.;
I ask this in Jesus' name.
Amen

(For those who have not accepted Jesus Christ as Lord and Saviour)

(Prayer)

Heavenly Father,
Lord, God Almighty,
I come humbly before you and acknowledge that I am a sinner in desperate need of a Saviour.
I confess with my mouth that Jesus is Lord;
And I believe in my heart that you raised you from the dead.
I ask you, O Lord;
To forgive all my sins and to cleanse me from all unrighteousness;
Come into my life and fill me with your Holy Spirit.
Teach me your ways and lead me in the right path.
Draw me to your Son, Jesus Christ that he may accept me as one of his;
For he said *"All that the Father giveth me shall come to me; and him that cometh to me I will in no wise cast out."*
Receive me, O Lord;
I ask, in Jesus' name;
Amen

PRAYER FOR MIRACLES

Message based on:

The Prayer of Jairus
and
The Prayer of the woman with the Issue of blood

The Prayer of Jairus

The Prayer of the woman with the Issue of blood

These prayers are combined in a message entitled:

Lay Hands on her that she may be healed

Mark Chapter 5:23
Jairus' daughter7

This message is based on the request that was made by a man named Jairus, a ruler of the synagogue whose daughter was at the point of death. Prior to this message, we took a historic walk through the country of the Gadarenes where Jesus encountered a man with an unclean spirit, but in fact, there were many spirits in the man; for when Jesus asked him his name, he replied, "Legion, for we are many."

And after driving out the spirits from the man, he gave him the directive to go back to his home and tell all the people what the Lord had done and how much compassion he had on him.

And so Jesus took his exit from that part of the country and sailed back to the other side of the sea only to be confronted by a multitude of people.

The work of the Lord is never done.

So we begin today's message on the other side of the sea.
I want you to open your Bibles to Mark Chapter 5 as we pick up the story from verse 21

The Bible says;
¶ And when Jesus was passed over again by ship unto the other side, much people gathered unto him: and he was nigh unto the sea.

22 And, behold, there cometh one of the rulers of the synagogue, Jairus by name; and when he saw him, he fell at his feet,

23 And besought him greatly, saying, My little daughter lieth at the point of death: *I pray thee*, come and lay thy hands on her, that she may be healed; and she shall live.

I want to use as a title for today's message;

"Lay hands on her, that she may be healed."

Father,
In Jesus' name I stand here before you and I ask you to stretch forth your hand and let your anointing be upon this word and upon everyone who is listening; and to those who are reading this book.
I pray that you would open their minds to understand the scriptures;
Open their hearts that they may attend unto the things which are spoken here today.
I ask it all in Jesus' name, and I give him all the praise and all the glory.
Amen.

Now, as you call tell from the words spoken by the ruler, Jairus that "the laying on of hands" must have been a common practice in Jesus' earthly ministry.
And may I say, it is still practiced today with great results.
Mark 16:18 says,
They shall lay hands on the sick, and they shall recover

So just to recap the story;

One of the rulers of the synagogue, Jairus by name; when he saw Jesus come out of the ship, he fell at his feet,
And begged him, saying, "My little daughter is lying in bed at the point of death: (*I am begging you*, please, please,) come and lay your hands on her, that she may be healed; and she shall live." (Mark 5:23)

Jesus raised Jairus' daughter from the dead

My friends
This request was founded on sheer love for his daughter. This man would
have done anything to save his daughter's life. A precious little girl of 12,
caught in the cross roads of death.
Why couldn't this ruler do something himself to save his child?
Why did he come to Jesus?

I'll tell you why;
There was no one else who had the power to save;
To heal, to cast out demons or even to raise the dead.
Acts 4:12 says;

"Neither is there salvation in any other: for there is none other name under
heaven given among men, whereby we must be saved." And that name is
Jesus of Nazareth, the Anointed one of God.

Remember what Mark 16:18 said;
"They shall lay hands on the sick, and they shall recover."

Watch this!

Look what happened as Jesus heads off to the house of Jairus where the little girl laid at the point of death.

My friend,

You have no idea what a distraction can do when a person is on a mission.

I'm sure you've been distracted before, and it may have cost you a lot; if not in time perhaps in money.

So what did take place at that crucial moment, as Jesus moved along this dusty road?

You will not believe it; if you were there, you would call it, 'outrageous.'

Listen to the story; the Bible says; (Mark 5:24-33)

²⁴And Jesus went with him; and much people followed him, and thronged him.

²⁵And a certain woman, which had an issue of blood twelve years,

²⁶And had suffered many things of many physicians, and had spent all that she had, and was nothing bettered, but rather grew worse,

²⁷When she had heard of Jesus, came in the press behind, and touched his garment.

²⁸For she said, If I may touch but his clothes, I shall be whole.

²⁹And straightway the fountain of her blood was dried up; and she felt in her body that she was healed of that plague.

³⁰And Jesus, immediately knowing in himself that virtue had gone out of him, turned him about in the press, and said, Who touched my clothes?

³¹And his disciples said unto him, Thou seest the multitude thronging thee, and sayest thou, Who touched me?

³²And he looked round about to see her that had done this thing.

[33]But the woman fearing and trembling, knowing what was done in her, came and fell down before him, and told him all the truth.

My friends,
Let me tell you something about this woman.
She was suffering with an issue of blood for 12 years;
And by the way, the little girl who lay dying was also 12 years old.
Was it a coincident, I don't know.
Now, if this woman was caught in public she could have been put away because she was considered unclean.

Allow me to let you expose a Leviticus law as it pertains to a woman and her monthly cycle.
(And I'm not talking about a bicycle that she rides once a month); but if you're old enough you will know what I mean.

This is what the law says; Leviticus 12:1-5;

[1]And the LORD spake unto Moses, saying,

[2]Speak unto the children of Israel, saying, If a woman have conceived seed, and born a man child: then she shall be unclean seven days; according to the days of the separation for her infirmity shall she be unclean.

[3]And in the eighth day the flesh of his foreskin shall be circumcised.

[4]And she shall then continue in the blood of her purifying three and thirty days; she shall touch no hallowed thing, nor come into the sanctuary, until the days of her purifying be fulfilled.

[5]But if she bear a maid child, then she shall be unclean two weeks, as in her separation: and she shall continue in the blood of her purifying threescore and six days.

So think for a moment and put yourself in that woman's position.
She has been unclean for 12 years;
Cannot go to church, cannot go to Bible College
Cannot go to Foundation classes

Cannot attend any Cell group meetings
She cannot go near anything that is sacred.
What a life; you're better off dead.

So she decided within herself, and concluded;
"I've had enough;
I'm going to put my life on the line;
I'm going to exercise my faith in whom I believe
I don't care anymore what they would do to me,
Even if I should be put away;
I'm going to give it my all.
The devil is not going to keep me down anymore;
I'm reaching out for Jesus.
The doctors have tried and they have failed;
Everyone I went to; gave me a bad report.

Well, this is the day the Lord hath made,
I'll rejoice and be glad in it. Hallelujah."

And that's when she decided to put her hands in the hand of the man from Galilee.
She got her victory; she got it; and she loved it;

Beloved;
You've got to turn it over to Jesus;
When the doctors say that there is nothing they can do;
You let them know that there is a doctor in the house named Jesus;
Whom God has anointed with power and the Holy Ghost;
Who's going around doing good and healing all those who are oppressed of the devil because God is with him. Hallelujah.

So Jesus looked at her;
And he said unto her, "Daughter, thy faith hath made thee whole; go in peace, and be whole of thy plague." (Mark 5:34)

So the distraction paid off for that woman; but what about the little girl?

Was she left there to die? What about her?

Is she going to make or is the poor child going to suffer as a result of the distraction?
Seems like a very long journey from the shore to Jairus' house.

Now the crowd is all stirred up;
They've seen the miracle of the woman with the issue of blood;
And I am sure there were many others in the crowd with some form of illness and wanted to be healed.

But watch this; verse 35 says,
"While he yet spake, there came from the ruler of the synagogue's house certain which said, Thy daughter is dead: why troublest thou the Master any further?"

When I read that part of the story, my suspicions were confirmed. I knew that would happen. Before I got to the end of this story, I felt that there would be some form of bad news in the making.

You see, I remembered what happened to a man named Lazarus in John Chapter 11.
The man was sick and they sent for Jesus; but Jesus took his time in coming;
And by the time he got to Bethany, the man was sleeping.
Let me put it a different way;
By the time he got to Bethany, his friend was dead.
I remembered that; and I thought that the same thing might have happened to that little girl.

Was I right? We'll soon find out.
The Bible went on to say in verses 36-40,

[36]As soon as Jesus heard the word that was spoken, he saith unto the ruler of the synagogue, Be not afraid, only believe.

[37]And he suffered no man to follow him, save Peter, and James, and John the brother of James.

[38]And he cometh to the house of the ruler of the synagogue, and seeth the tumult, and them that wept and wailed greatly.

³⁹And when he was come in, he saith unto them, Why make ye this ado, and weep? the damsel is not dead, but sleepeth.

⁴⁰And they laughed him to scorn. But when he had put them all out, he taketh the father and the mother of the damsel, and them that were with him, and entereth in where the damsel was lying.

Let me pause for a moment to say this;
If you're going to pray for someone, especially for someone who is sick;
Do not take anyone who does not believe.
Satan can use them as a stronghold to try and negate the miracle.
When you come together in prayer, you must come believing.

In John 20:27 Jesus said to Thomas;
"Reach hither thy finger, and behold my hands; and reach hither thy hand, and thrust it into my side: and be not faithless, but believing."
Beloved, you've got to have faith.
The Bible says in Hebrews 11:6 says;
"But without faith it is impossible to please him: for he that cometh to God must believe that he is, and that he is a rewarder of them that diligently seek him."
James 1:6 says;
You have to ask in faith, nothing wavering. For he that wavers is like a wave of the sea driven with the wind and tossed.
Let not that man think that he shall receive anything of the Lord.
A double-minded man is unstable in all his ways.

You're got to believe.
This is serious. It's a matter of Life and death. Mark 5:41-43 says,

⁴¹And he took the damsel by the hand, and said unto her, Talitha cumi; which is, being interpreted, Damsel, I say unto thee, arise.

⁴²And straightway the damsel arose, and walked; for she was of the age of twelve years. And they were astonished with a great astonishment.

⁴³And he charged them straitly that no man should know it; and commanded that something should be given her to eat.

So to summarize;
The little girl did die;
But Jesus! Hallelujah
He raised her from the dead.
And even so will he raise us up from the dead when he comes again.
But you must have faith in God and in Jesus Christ.
You must believe in order to receive.
If you're not a Christian and you feel the prompting in your heart, don't resist it;
It is the Holy Spirit.
The Bible says that no one can come unto Jesus except it were given unto him of the Father. *(John 6:65)*

So I urge you to do the right thing;
Receive Jesus as Your Savior and Lord.
He died on the cross for your sins and rose again on the third day.
He's alive and well;
Seated at the right hand of God the Father with all power and might.

My friends,
Who do you think saved a wretch like me?
Yes, It is Jesus;
And by a simple prayer you can receive him into your life, if you haven't done so already. When you say this prayer, you will receive a new life;
You will be Born-Again.

This simple prayer is so powerful, it can and will change your life for ever;

Prayer

Heavenly Father,
I come before you and ask you to forgive me of my sins.
I believe that Jesus died on the cross for my sins;
And rose again on the third day;
So with my mouth, I confess the Lord Jesus,
And I believe in my heart that God raised him from the dead;
So according to Romans 10:9 which is your promise;
I am saved. Hallelujah.

My time is up and I have to go now;
But write and tell us what God has done for you today.
Amen.

Email: thegateway2heaven@yahoo.com

Notes

FAITH AND PRAYER

Mark 11:24

What things soever ye desire, when ye pray,
Believe that ye receive them,
And ye shall have them.

Faith and Prayer

Faith and Prayer is as **Vitamin D and Calcium.** Just as calcium needs vitamin D to be effective in the body, prayer needs faith in order to obtain the answers to the petitions. Mark 11:24, Jesus said, "Therefore I say unto you, *What things soever ye desire, when ye pray believe that ye receive them, and ye shall have them.*

1 John 5:14-15 says, "*And this is the confidence that we have in him that, if we ask any thing according to his will, he heareth us:*

[15]And if we know that he hear us, whatsoever we ask, we know that we have the petitions that we desired of him."

These two scriptures give us an indication as to how important faith is, when we pray. Faith is also important when we listen to the Word of God. Hebrews 4:2 says, "*For unto us was the gospel preached, as well as unto them: but the word preached did not profit them, not being mixed with faith in them that heard it."*

So we can conclude that faith is the key both to success and prosperity; and above all, the way to God's heart. Hebrews 11:1 says, "*Now faith is the substance of things hoped for, the evidence of things not seen."* Verse 6 says, "*But without faith it is impossible to please him: for he that cometh to God must believe that he is, and that he is a rewarder of them that diligently seek him."*

God loves when we ask in faith and respond in faith. There is a saying; 'Fear creeps but faith leaps; fear hesitates but faith accelerates.' James 2:18 says, "*Yea, a man may say, Thou hast faith, and I have works: shew me thy faith without thy works, and I will shew thee my faith by my works."* There has to be a corresponding action to your faith. Faith must not stand alone; it must be integrated with your **asking,** your **hearing**, your **actions,** your **speaking,** and your **prayers.**

Let us examine **faith and asking.** Asking can be a form of prayer when voiced to God; but a request when addressed to man. In both instances one must still ask in faith. If you are asking a person for something and you convey a sense of negativity or rejection, you are not likely to receive your request. It is the same with God. James 1:5-8 says, "*If any of you lack* *wisdom, let him ask of God, that giveth to all men liberally, and upbraideth not; and it shall be given him.*

⁶But let him ask in faith, nothing wavering. For he that wavereth is like a wave of the sea driven with the wind and tossed.

⁷For let not that man think that he shall receive any thing of the Lord.

⁸A double minded man is unstable in all his ways."

When we ask, whether in prayer to God or in request to man, we must not waver because a wavering man is a man that vacillates and he is unstable in all his ways. There is hardly anyone who would like to do business with a man that vacillates and unstable in all his ways. Even God refuses to answer his requests.

Faith and hearing: Jesus made a very profound statement concerning our hearing which can be detrimental if not adhered to. These are his words as recorded in the book of Revelation, Chapter 3, verses 20-22; *"Behold, I stand at the door, and knock: if any man hear my voice, and open the door, I will come in to him, and will sup with him, and he with me.*

²¹To him that overcometh will I grant to sit with me in my throne, even as I also overcame, and am set down with my Father in his throne.

²²He that hath an ear, let him hear what the Spirit saith unto the churches."

Jesus is asking for an invitation to fellowship with any man who would hear his voice and invite him in. The problem lies in the inability to hear his call. This is why faith and hearing must be mixed in order to hear that call to eternal life. The Bible emphatically says in Romans 10:17 says, *"So then faith cometh by hearing, and hearing by the Word of God."* The Word of God is the prescription to restoring our ability to hear the voice of God. Romans 10:14 says, *"How then shall they call on him in whom they have not believed? and how shall they believe in him of whom they have not heard? and how shall they hear without a preacher?"*

The Word of God must first be preached and those who are **willing** to surrender to the Lordship of Jesus Christ will receive his anointing that comes by the Holy Spirit; then will they hear the voice of God. Hebrews 4:2 says, *"For unto us was the gospel preached, as well as unto them: but the word preached did not profit them, not being mixed with faith in them that heard it."* Again, we see in this scripture that faith was necessary for one to profit from the Word of God.

How many of us have heard some news that we did not believe? Even Thomas did not believe the news that Jesus was risen from the dead (John 20:24-25). However, if the one who is reporting the news is credible, we are apt to believe. I said that to say this, the bible is an undeniable credible source of information about God's plan of salvation and how that plan was executed by Jesus Christ when he died on the cross for the sin of the world.

Since faith comes by hearing and hearing by the Word of God; then faith comes by Jesus Christ because he is the Word of God. John 1:1 says, *"In the beginning was the Word, and the Word was with God, and the Word was God."* He is also the author and finisher of our faith (Hebrews 12:2). He promised in John 14:12, *"Verily, verily, I say unto you, He that believeth on me, the works that I do shall he do also; and greater works than these shall he do; because I go unto my Father."* Faith in Jesus Christ will give the believer the ability to do greater works; with the exception of the work of salvation which is done once and for all and made known by Jesus when he said, *"It is finished"* (John 19:30).

So the hearing produces the faith; and the faith produces the action. Let's talk about faith and action.

Faith and actions: The bible says in James 2:26, *"For as the body without the spirit is dead, so faith without works is dead also."* In order for faith to work for the glory of God, we must be in communion with the author of our faith, Jesus Christ. The way we commune with Jesus Christ, is through prayer and worship; as well as doing those things which he commanded us to do; such as feeding the hungry, giving drink to the thirsty, clothing the naked, visiting the sick, and visiting those in prison (Matthew 25:35-36).

Our actions speak louder than words; but in some situations, our words can produce mighty actions that can only be attributed to the power of God. 1 John 3:17-18 says, *"But whoso hath this world's good, and seeth his brother have need, and shutteth up his bowels of compassion from him, how dwelleth the love of God in him?*

18My little children, let us not love in word, neither in tongue; but in deed and in truth." While it is true that we should not just speak love but demonstrate it by our deeds; Jesus demonstrated his deeds of love by what he spoke; and what he spoke is what he did. For example, he **said** in John 15:13-14**,** *"Greater love hath no man than this, that a man lay down his life for his friends. Ye are my friends, if ye do whatsoever I command you."* In John 19:17-18 Jesus died on the cross for his friends; just as he said, and not only for his friends but for the sin of the world that whosoever believeth in him would not perish but have eternal life. In John 10:17, he said, *"Therefore doth my Father love me, because I lay down my life, that I might take it again.*

18No man taketh it from me, but I lay it down of myself. I have power to lay it down, and I have power to take it again. This commandment have I received of my Father."

Romans 5:8 says, *"But God commendeth his love toward us, in that, while we were yet sinners, Christ died for us."* That was the greatest demonstration of God's love for us. He continues to demonstrate his love by his word which is displayed on the pages of the bible. His word is given to us that we may meditate on it; internalize it; and speak it boldly for the cause of good and the advancement of the kingdom of God; and at the same time to the deprivation of evil.

Faith and speaking: What should we say when we speak? There is an array of things that we can say when we speak; but the one thing that we should no speak is clearly stated in Ephesians 4:9 which says, *"Let no corrupt communication proceed out of your mouth, but that which is good to the use of edifying, that it may minister grace unto the hearers."* One might argue that the conversation which Jesus had with the fig tree was a corrupt communication because it resulted in destruction; but on the contrary, it demonstrated the power of faith in the spoken word. Matthew 21:18-22 tells it this way, *"Now in the morning as he returned into the city, he hungered.*

19And when he saw a fig tree in the way, he came to it, and found nothing thereon, but leaves only, and said unto it, Let no fruit grow on thee henceforward for ever. And presently the fig tree withered away.

20And when the disciples saw it, they marvelled, saying, How soon is the fig tree withered away!

²¹Jesus answered and said unto them, Verily I say unto you, If ye have faith, and doubt not, ye shall not only do this which is done to the fig tree, but also if ye shall say unto this mountain, Be thou removed, and be thou cast into the sea; it shall be done.

²²And all things, whatsoever ye shall ask in prayer, believing, ye shall receive."

The incident was a faith building exercise that would prove valuable to the disciples in the course of their ministry. When Jesus spoke, his words were faith filled words that ministered grace and healing to the people. When he spoke to Jairus concerning his daughter who was dead, the man received hope. Mark 5:36, Jesus said to Jairus, *"Be not afraid, only believe."*

To the woman with the issue of blood, he said, *"Daughter, thy faith hath made thee whole; go in peace, and be whole of thy plague* (Mark 5:34). When the great storm of wind arose at sea while the disciples were in the boat, his words were, *"Peace, be still."*

To the servants at the wedding in Cana of Galilee, he said, *"Fill the waterpots with water; draw out and bear unto the governor of the feast."* Miraculously the water was turned into the best wine.

Everything that Jesus did was done knowing that it would be done as he said. In John 5:19-20, Jesus said to the multitude concerning the words he had spoken to a cripple man and made him whole. The bible says, *"Then answered Jesus and said unto them, Verily, verily, I say unto you, The Son can do nothing of himself, but what he seeth the Father do: for what things soever he doeth, these also doeth the Son likewise.*

²⁰For the Father loveth the Son, and sheweth him all things that himself doeth: and he will shew him greater works than these, that ye may marvel." Jesus always encouraged his disciples to speak with faith; say to the mountain, "Be thou removed." Speak to the evil spirits and cast them out! Doing the will of God and speaking in faith will always bring positive results on the situation that's before you. Speaking in faith and inviting the Lord in the situation is the perfect setting for a prayer meeting. Matthew 18:19-20 says, *"That if two of you shall agree on earth as touching any thing that they shall ask, it shall be done for them of my Father which is in heaven.*

²⁰For where two or three are gathered together in my name, there am I in the midst of them."

Faith and prayers: Faith, as described in the bible, is the substance of things hoped for, the evidence of things not seen. It also says that without faith, it is impossible to please God. Prayer on the other hand is asking or communicating with God that we may develop intimacy with him. When we put faith and prayer together, we then have the substance of what we are asking for; and the evidence of it; though we haven't yet seen it. We believe that we have it. The idea of receiving your prayer request is echoed throughout the gospel. In Mark 11:24, Jesus said, *"Therefore I say unto you, What things soever ye desire, when ye pray, believe that ye receive them, and ye shall have them."*

In 1 John 5:14, John said, "And this is the confidence that we have in him, that, if we ask any thing according to his will, he heareth us:

[15]And if we know that he hear us, whatsoever we ask, we know that we have the petitions that we desired of him."

There are times when we find ourselves in a dire situation and our world is literally crumbling before our eyes; and we are left with no other choice but to stretch our faith to the limit. That's the time when we call out to God, in desperation, hoping against all odds that he is listening to our prayers. But if we read what the bible says in 1 John 5:14-15, we don't have to feel the desperation that comes with fear. In that desperation our faith begins to waver and that displeases God; as we read in James 1:5-8. Fear may be described as faith becoming contaminated as the thoughts of unbelief persist. We are to cast those thoughts down (2 Corinthians 10:5) and believe that God is able to meet all your need in Christ Jesus ((Philippians 4:19)

Everyone who prays, usually begin with the notion that God is listening; and if he is listening, he does hear the prayers because God is not deaf; but sometimes the prayers are not answered. The problem begins when our prayers are not in line with the will of God for our lives. James 5:14-15 says, *"If we pray and ask according to his will, he hears us."* Some people pray for things that are contrary to the word of God. For example; someone would pray for God to take someone's life. That prayer could not be answered because Jesus said in John 10:10, *"The thief cometh not, but for to steal, and to kill, and to destroy: I am come that they might have life, and that they might have it more abundantly."* Another example is someone who prays to be joined with another who is not a Christian. The bible clearly states in 2

Corinthians 6:14, "*Be ye not unequally yoked together with unbelievers: for what fellowship hath righteousness with unrighteousness? and what communion hath light with darkness?*"

So there are prayers that God will not answer even though they may be said in faith. There are prayers that God will not answer because of your spiritual condition. For example; If you have a contention with a brother, be reconciled with him first, then come to the altar of God and offer your gifts (Matthew 5:23-24).

Sin can also prevent God from answering your prayer even though they may be offered in faith. 2 Chronicles 7:14-15 says, "*If my people, which are called by my name, shall humble themselves, and pray, and seek my face, and turn from their wicked ways; then will I hear from heaven, and will forgive their sin, and will heal their land.*

[15]Now mine eyes shall be open, and mine ears attent unto the prayer that is made in this place."

God takes no pleasure in sin. Sin is an abomination to God and anyone who knowingly withholds sin from the Lord and refuses to confess them will not reap the blessings of the Lord. It makes no difference if that person has faith to move mountains, the Lord will not be impressed. 1 Corinthians 13:2 says, "*And though I have the gift of prophecy, and understand all mysteries, and all knowledge; and though I have all faith, so that I could remove mountains, and have not charity, I am nothing.*" When we understand the relationship between God and Love; and know that love is not a part of God, but that God is love, we will see the importance and the necessity of exercising love in all that we do and say. When we pray, love must be the centerpiece of our prayers. In order for our prayers to be lifted up in faith, there must be love because faith works by love (Galatians 5:6).

Notes

PRAYER OF REPENTANCE

The Lost Son

The Lost Son

Luke 15:11-24

The Parable of the lost son is a reflection of a lost and dying world that needs to repent before the Lord for all the wrong that's being done. In this parable, Jesus goes to great length to explain what it sometimes takes for a sinner to come to the realization that he needs a Saviour. The prayer that is rehearsed by the lost son (Luke 15:18-1.9) is not intercessory by any means, but a direct, one-on-one prayer of repentance from a soul that was near the point of death. Such prayers most often reflect the brokenness of the person's spirit, and thus capture the heart of God.

The passage is listed here for convenience:

Luke 15:11-24 (King James Version)

[11] And he said, A certain man had two sons:

[12] And the younger of them said to his father, Father, give me the portion of goods that falleth to me. And he divided unto them his living.

[13] And not many days after the younger son gathered all together, and took his journey into a far country, and there wasted his substance with riotous living.

[14] And when he had spent all, there arose a mighty famine in that land; and he began to be in want.

[15] And he went and joined himself to a citizen of that country; and he sent him into his fields to feed swine.

[16] And he would fain have filled his belly with the husks that the swine did eat: and no man gave unto him.

[17] And when he came to himself, he said, How many hired servants of my father's have bread enough and to spare, and I perish with hunger!

[18] I will arise and go to my father, and will say unto him, Father, I have sinned against heaven, and before thee,

¹⁹And am no more worthy to be called thy son: make me as one of thy hired servants.

²⁰And he arose, and came to his father. But when he was yet a great way off, his father saw him, and had compassion, and ran, and fell on his neck, and kissed him.

²¹And the son said unto him, Father, I have sinned against heaven, and in thy sight, and am no more worthy to be called thy son.

²²But the father said to his servants, Bring forth the best robe, and put it on him; and put a ring on his hand, and shoes on his feet:

²³And bring hither the fatted calf, and kill it; and let us eat, and be merry:

²⁴For this my son was dead, and is alive again; he was lost, and is found. And they began to be merry.

The Lost son, sometimes referred to as the Prodigal son is not necessarily a corrupted or delinquent son; for he appeared to have been raised up in a 'well-to-do' home; with authority over a number of servants. He was also fortunate to have an older brother who is also part of the story. So what would cause such a privileged person to abandon the comfort and security of his father's home and venture out into a far country that was filled with deception and all forms of immorality that could ruin his name and his reputation? According to the parable, all of those things happened to the young man and he was left with no alternative but to reach to the one he knew loved him. In so doing, he rehearsed a prayer to the father that I consider to be one of the most effectual prayers of repentance. It may be a short prayer but it encapsulates what the bible teaches about the salvation of the world through Jesus Christ.

When Jesus spoke of the lost, one can be assured that he also included the solution of how to be saved. The method by which the lost son was restored was through repentance. There is a position that some people take when they are faced with the prospect of being separated from God forever. They tend to procrastinate until it is too late to make the right decision. For instance, the rich man and Lazarus as told in Luke chapter 16:19-31. Verse 24 says, *"And he (the rich man) cried and said, Father Abraham, have mercy on me, and send Lazarus, that he may dip the tip of his finger in water, and cool my tongue; for I am tormented in this flame."*

Now realizing the consequences for not trusting in the Lord, and that it was too late to change his fate; he offered another prayer; not of repentance but intercession. Verses 27-28 says, *"Then he said, I pray thee therefore, father, that thou wouldest send him to my father's house;*

For I have five brothers; that he may testify unto them, lest they also come into this place of torment."

His prayer was well constructed; first he cried for mercy then made his requests. He also included an intercessory prayer for his brothers' salvation; but it was too late. Someone once asked me if the souls that went to hell could pray for their desires; and without hesitation, I directed them to this parable. The prayers that were offered by the rich man in the fires of hell were never answered and will never be answered; but those offered by the lost son even while he was among the pigs; in his deepest state of despair led him to make the right decision and return to the father. There can be no true repentance without a personal relationship with the Father through Jesus Christ.

Let us examine the prayer of repentance that was offered by the lost son:

Matthew 15:18-19, "I will arise and go to my father, and will say unto him, Father I have sinned against heaven, and before thee;

And am no more worthy to be called thy son; make me as one of thy hired servants."

1. **He decided to take action and return to the father.**
2. **He made a conscious decision to confess his sins to the father.**
3. **He was willing to humble himself before the Father.**
4. **He was willing to be a servant.**

What he did last, he should have done first; and what he did first, he should not have done at all. His decision to confess his sins was the wisest decision of all. The bible says in 1 John 1:9, *"If we confess our sins, he is faithful and just to forgive us our sins, and to cleanse us from all unrighteousness."*

He was also willing to humble himself before the father as he repented was another great step in the right direction. James 4:7-10 says, "*Submit yourselves therefore to God. Resist the devil, and he will flee from you.*

8Draw nigh to God, and he will draw nigh to you. Cleanse your hands, ye sinners; and purify your hearts, ye double minded.

9Be afflicted, and mourn, and weep: let your laughter be turned to mourning, and your joy to heaviness.

10Humble yourselves in the sight of the Lord, and he shall lift you up."

1 Peter 5:6-7 echoes the same message, "*Humble yourselves therefore under the mighty hand of God, that he may exalt you in due time:*

7Casting all your care upon him; for he careth for you."

Every word from that prayer which the lost son had rehearsed, he voiced in the presence of his father. But the father, being so overwhelmed with joy at the return of his son, was more concerned about blessing him for making such a wise decision. This is what the prayer of repentance can do. It causes the entire heavenly host to explode with rejoicing. Luke 15:7 Jesus said, "*I say unto you, that likewise joy shall be in heaven over one sinner that repenteth, more than over ninety and nine just persons, which need no repentance.*"

The call to repentance is a message that resounds throughout the bible. The Prophets and the Apostles have pleaded with the people to come before the Lord and repent of their sins.
For example:

Ezekiel 14:6 "*Therefore say unto the house of Israel, Thus saith the Lord GOD; Repent, and turn yourselves from your idols; and turn away your faces from all your abominations.*"

Matthew 3:2 says, "*And saying, Repent ye: for the kingdom of heaven is at hand.*"

Acts 2:38 says, "*Then Peter said unto them, Repent, and be baptized every one of you in the name of Jesus Christ for the remission of sins, and ye shall receive the gift of the Holy Ghost.*"

Revelation 3:19 says, "*As many as I love, I rebuke and chasten: be zealous therefore, and repent.*"

The message is clear; God wants us to repent of our sins and become re-united with him through Jesus Christ, our Lord. When we come before the Father, and express our desires, in the authority of the name of Jesus Christ, we will get his attention. The next chapter is focused on asking in the name of Jesus.

Notes

Notes

CHAPTER THREE

The Prayer of Jesus

John 17
John 11
Luke 22

THE PRAYER OF JESUS

John 17

Who he prayed for and what he prayed for:

For himself (Verses 1-5)

For the disciples (Verses 6-19)

For future believers (verse 20)

For the unity of the church (verses 21-26)

John 17

For himself (Verses 1-5)

John Chapter 17 outlines the prayer of Jesus which has been classified by most theologians as the greatest of all prayers recorded in the bible; and this does not in any way undermine the prayer he taught his disciples in Luke chapter 11; commonly referred to as 'the Lord's prayer.'

In this personal yet intercessory prayer, Jesus made four distinct requests of the Lord which can be adopted as a guideline for our own prayers to the Father. First he prayed for himself; then for his disciples. He followed that with a prayer for future believers and then concluded with a prayer for the unity of them all. Let us examine the prayer he offered for himself and determine what guidelines we can apply when we make our petitions to the Father.

John Chapter 17, verses 1-5 is listed here for convenience:

¹These words spake Jesus, and lifted up his eyes to heaven, and said, Father, the hour is come; glorify thy Son, that thy Son also may glorify thee:

²As thou hast given him power over all flesh, that he should give eternal life to as many as thou hast given him.

³And this is life eternal, that they might know thee the only true God, and Jesus Christ, whom thou hast sent.

⁴I have glorified thee on the earth: I have finished the work which thou gavest me to do.

⁵And now, O Father, glorify thou me with thine own self with the glory which I had with thee before the world was.

The bible teaches in James 5:16 that we must pray for one another; but we are also taught by Jesus himself that we must ask the Father for the desires of our heart. In Matthew 7:11 he said, *"Ask, and it shall be given you; seek, and ye shall find; knock, and it shall be opened unto you:*

⁸For every one that asketh receiveth; and he that seeketh findeth; and to him that knocketh it shall be opened.

⁹Or what man is there of you, whom if his son ask bread, will he give him a stone?

¹⁰Or if he ask a fish, will he give him a serpent?

¹¹If ye then, being evil, know how to give good gifts unto your children, how much more shall your Father which is in heaven give good things to them that ask him?"

When Jesus began his petition, he did not commence with an intercessory prayer for the disciples; but rather a personal prayer for his glorification. When we examine this section of the prayer, we can also conclude that it was intercessory in nature because he referred to himself as thy Son; and also used the pronoun 'him' instead of 'me.' It actually appeared as if he was asking for God's Son to be glorified and not really himself. For example, listen to what the elder brother in the story of the lost son said to his father. Luke 15:29-32, *"And he answering said to his father, Lo, these many years do I serve thee, neither transgressed I at any time thy commandment: and yet thou never gavest me a kid, that I might make merry with my friends:*

³⁰But as soon as this thy son was come, which hath devoured thy living with harlots, thou hast killed for him the fatted calf.

³¹And he said unto him, Son, thou art ever with me, and all that I have is thine.

³²It was meet that we should make merry, and be glad: for this thy brother was dead, and is alive again; and was lost, and is found."

He referred to his own brother as thy son and not my brother. They were the same person but temporally he divorced himself from the relationship and considered the brother another individual. Perhaps it was the same with Jesus when he petitioned the Father on his own behalf; saying, "glorify thy Son, that thy Son also may glorify thee;" Verse 5 adds a little clarity to the idea of this being an intercessory prayer in the first part, for Jesus then spoke clearly of himself as the one who was requesting to be glorified. He said, *"And now, O Father, glorify thou **me** with thine own self with the glory which **I** had with thee before the world was."*

So initially, he was as one asking for glory for another; and then as one asking for glory for himself. This would not be significant for us as we pray unless we were seeking the power of the anointing which had become inoperative through disobedience; in which case, we would be interceding for the person who once operated in the anointing to have that power again; knowing fully well that the person is you.

Jesus was doing first things first. He did the job that the Father entrusted him to do; and soon it would be time for him to return to the Father. Since he had divested himself of all the glory which he had from before the world existed; it seemed fit for him to once again be clothed with the same glory which he had back then. So what are we to gather from this Godly request? There are times when we have to debase ourselves, or give up all that we have in order to carry out the will of God; but when the task is completed, we can feel confident that we will be rewarded double for our trouble. Mark 10:28-30 talks about the reward that is given to those who forsake themselves for the Kingdom of God. This is what it says; *"Then Peter began to say unto him, Lo, we have left all, and have followed thee.*

[29]And Jesus answered and said, Verily I say unto you, There is no man that hath left house, or brethren, or sisters, or father, or mother, or wife, or children, or lands, for my sake, and the gospel's,

[30]But he shall receive an hundredfold now in this time, houses, and brethren, and sisters, and mothers, and children, and lands, with persecutions; and in the world to come eternal life."

In the case of Jesus, he had the glory but gave it up and chose to be crucified on a cross that we in turn may be glorified through his death, burial, resurrection and ascension. When we come before the Father in prayer, we can take this procedure to another dimension because we come in the name of Jesus and not in our own name or any other name. The bible says in Acts 4:12, *"Neither is there salvation in any other; for there is none other name under heaven given among men whereby we must be saved."* That name is Jesus, the Anointed. As a result of that name and the power and authority it carries, we are able as the bible says in Hebrews 4:16, *"Let us therefore come boldly unto the throne of grace, that we may obtain mercy, and find grace to help in time of need."* When we therefore come before the throne of grace, we receive the unmerited favour of God and all his forgiveness that we may return to our assignments expressing that love and forgiving others who trespass against.

When we come before the Father, as Jesus did, we need to acknowledge him for who he is and what he has done for us; the power which he has given us through the use of the name of Jesus. We must thank him for all the blessings with which he has blessed us; even in heavenly places in Christ Jesus; and never ever be ashamed to proclaim the deity of Jesus Christ, the love of God and the sweet fellowship of the Holy Spirit.

Jesus prayed for himself that he may be glorified that he may in turn glorify the Father. Whatever we ask for it should be something that would bring praise, honour and glory to the Lord Jesus Christ. Jesus continued his prayer which was undoubtedly intercessory because it was for their protection and a sacred unity.

John 17

For the disciples (Verses 6-19)

As parents, we always pray for the protection of our loved one. That is the role of a parent, but sometimes we neglect to fulfill that role and our children fall prey to the enemy of their soul. Jesus however never lapsed as he watches over us; for he keeps us in continuous prayer; interceding day and night on our behalf. Hebrews 7:25 says, *"Wherefore he is able also to save them to the uttermost that come unto God by him, seeing he ever liveth to make intercession for them."*

Romans 8:26 says, *"Likewise the Spirit also helpeth our infirmities: for we know not what we should pray for as we ought: but the Spirit itself maketh intercession for us with groanings which cannot be uttered."*

I will say this again; "we must pray one for another." We do not necessarily have to know the person that we are praying for; because the body of Christ extends all across the world even to places that we have never visited; but to love them and pray for them is the will of God for our lives.

John 17:6-19 is listed here for convenience:

"⁶I have manifested thy name unto the men which thou gavest me out of the world: thine they were, and thou gavest them me; and they have kept thy word.

⁷Now they have known that all things whatsoever thou hast given me are of thee.

⁸For I have given unto them the words which thou gavest me; and they have received them, and have known surely that I came out from thee, and they have believed that thou didst send me.

⁹I pray for them: I pray not for the world, but for them which thou hast given me; for they are thine.

¹⁰And all mine are thine, and thine are mine; and I am glorified in them.

¹¹And now I am no more in the world, but these are in the world, and I come to thee. Holy Father, keep through thine own name those whom thou hast given me, that they may be one, as we are.

¹²While I was with them in the world, I kept them in thy name: those that thou gavest me I have kept, and none of them is lost, but the son of perdition; that the scripture might be fulfilled.

¹³And now come I to thee; and these things I speak in the world, that they might have my joy fulfilled in themselves.

¹⁴I have given them thy word; and the world hath hated them, because they are not of the world, even as I am not of the world.

¹⁵I pray not that thou shouldest take them out of the world, but that thou shouldest keep them from the evil.

16They are not of the world, even as I am not of the world.

17Sanctify them through thy truth: thy word is truth.

18As thou hast sent me into the world, even so have I also sent them into the world.

19And for their sakes I sanctify myself, that they also might be sanctified through the truth."

In this prayer, Jesus alerted the Father that he was not praying for the world but for those whom he had given to him. This does not necessarily mean that Jesus was only talking about the disciples; but it had far greater implications; especially when we test this saying against what he said in John 3:16, *"For God so loved the world, that he gave his only begotten Son, that whosoever believeth in him should not perish, but have everlasting life."* And again in John 1:12 which says, *"But as many as received him, to them gave he power to become the sons of God, even to them that believe on his name."* These verses clearly refer to people other than the disciples. They refer to '**Whosoever**' as indicated in John 3:16 and '**As many**' as we noticed in John 1:12. So if we are to use this section of the prayer as a guideline, we must therefore extend our intercession beyond our family and close friend and reach out to all the body of Christ around the world.

Jesus also prayed for their unity in verse 11; and their protection in verse 12. In verse 14 Jesus tells the Father of the persecution of his disciples because of their allegiance to the word of God. It was not that God did not know what had taken place; but it was important for Jesus to communicate with the Father concerning those things. Even though Jesus was concerned about the well being of his disciples, he never wanted to remove them from the world. He asked the Father to sanctify them through his truth, which is the word of God (John 17:17). The word 'sanctify' means to set apart; and Jesus wanted the Father to set the disciples apart to continue the work of God. He also set himself apart for the sake of the disciples. Jesus would not ask you to do something that he himself would not do. So he continued to pray indirectly for the unbelievers (John 17:20).

John 17

For future believers

John 17:20 is listed here for convenience:

"Neither pray I for these alone, but for them also which shall believe on me through their word;"

It would seem counter productive for Jesus to pray only for the disciples when he was about to be crucified for the sin of the world and opening the way for all to be reconciled to God. If the disciples were all he cared about, why would he die on a cross to redeem the world? If would have been easier to take them out of the world and save himself from the cross. If the cross was for the salvation of all humanity then prayer must be offered up as our way of pleading that God would draw them to his Son. John 6:65 says, "*Therefore said I unto you, that no man can come unto me, except it were given unto him of my Father.*" When Moses divided the Red Sea to allow the Israelites to escape from Pharaoh's army (Exodus 14:21-31), it would have been counter productive if he had not closed the sea again. When Jesus died on the cross for the salvation of the world, it would have been counter productive if there was no way for the world to know, to understand, to believe and accept the sacrifice he made. Therefore the word of God is the key to open the door to a new life in Christ. Our prayers and supplications are very important; for even as he listens to Jesus, he also listens to us. Romans 10:13-15 says, *"13For whosoever shall call upon the name of the Lord shall be saved.*
14How then shall they call on him in whom they have not believed? and how shall they believe in him of whom they have not heard? and how shall they hear without a preacher?
15And how shall they preach, except they be sent? as it is written, How beautiful are the feet of them that preach the gospel of peace, and bring glad tidings of good things!"

John 17

For the unity of the church

John 17:21-26 is listed here for convenience:

"²¹That they all may be one; as thou, Father, art in me, and I in thee, that they also may be one in us: that the world may believe that thou hast sent me.

²²And the glory which thou gavest me I have given them; that they may be one, even as we are one:

²³I in them, and thou in me, that they may be made perfect in one; and that the world may know that thou hast sent me, and hast loved them, as thou hast loved me.

²⁴Father, I will that they also, whom thou hast given me, be with me where I am; that they may behold my glory, which thou hast given me: for thou lovedst me before the foundation of the world.

²⁵O righteous Father, the world hath not known thee: but I have known thee, and these have known that thou hast sent me.

*²⁶And I have declared unto them thy name, and will de*clare it: that the love wherewith thou hast loved me may be in them, and I in them."

Jesus concluded his prayer by revisiting the subject of unity. The saying 'United we stand, divided we fall' is indeed a wise saying. Jesus understood the importance of unity and what it meant from an organizational point of view and spiritual unity as it applies to the kingdom of God. In an address to the Pharisees concerning the power of God and the Holy Spirit, he made a profound statement which can be found in Matthew 12:25-30 which says, *"And Jesus knew their thoughts, and said unto them, Every kingdom divided against itself is brought to desolation; and every city or house divided against itself shall not stand:*

[26]And if Satan cast out Satan, he is divided against himself; how shall then his kingdom stand?

[27]And if I by Beelzebub cast out devils, by whom do your children cast them out? therefore they shall be your judges.

[28]But if I cast out devils by the Spirit of God, then the kingdom of God is come unto you.

[29]Or else how can one enter into a strong man's house, and spoil his goods, except he first bind the strong man? and then he will spoil his house.

[30]He that is not with me is against me; and he that gathereth not with me scattereth abroad."

Jesus and the Father had an intimate relationship; and that's the kind of relationship he wants to have with us. He wants us to be united as the body of Christ and together be united with him and the Father. In John 14:23 he said to his disciples, *"If a man love me, he will keep my words; and my Father will love him, and we will come unto him, and make our abode with him."* Jesus wants us to be in unity with each other because he died not for one but for all. He wants us to abide in him as he abides in the Father. In John 14:10, he responded to Philip's request by saying, *"Believest thou not that I am in the Father, and the Father in me? the words that I speak unto you I speak not of myself: but the Father that dwelleth in me, he doeth the works."* That was Jesus' prayer and it should be ours also. Before Jesus prayed that prayer, he made a promise to his disciples and to all who would believe in him. That promise is found in John 14:2-3 which says, *"In my Father's house are many mansions: if it were not so, I would have told you. I go to prepare a place for you.*

[3]And if I go and prepare a place for you, I will come again, and receive you unto myself; that where I am, there ye may be also."

Here is a simple prayer to let the Father know that you trust in him and in his Son Jesus Christ and the Holy Spirit.

Father, I thank you for the sacrificial gift of your Son Jesus Christ who died on the cross for my sins and the sins of all the world.

I confess Jesus as Lord and Saviour of my life and believe that you raised him from the dead; and he is alive and well and in your presence.

I also believe that he will fulfill all the promises he had made in the Holy Bible.

I look forward to the day of his return when I shall be with him forever.

Amen.

John 11:41-42

For the raising of Lazarus from the dead

It is true that Jesus spent a lot of time in prayer to the Father; but he was not in the habit of asking the Father to perform any miracles for the people. The bible says that *'God anointed Jesus of Nazareth with the Holy Ghost and with power; who went about doing good, and healing all that were oppressed of the devil; for God was with him.'* So He had the power and the authority to heal the sick, raise the dead, cast out devils, feed the hungry and any good that he wish to bestow upon the people. However there was a time when he actually prayed to the Father, in the presence of the people; but that was done to instill in their hearts that the Father had indeed sent Jesus for the salvation of the world.

The prayer would enlighten the people concerning Jesus and the Father, and at the same time cause their faith in him to be lifted up to another dimension. After all, the miracle that was about to take place was the watershed of Jesus' ministry. The power and reality of a future resurrection of the dead weighed heavily on the results of Jesus' prayer and subsequent action.

The prayer was a simple one and it formed the basis for the teaching of the Apostle John concerning the answers to our prayers. 1 John 5:14-15 says, *"And this is the confidence that we have in him, that, if we ask any thing according to his will, he heareth us:*

[15]And if we know that he hear us, whatsoever we ask, we know that we have the petitions that we desired of him."

Knowing that God has heard your prayer gives you the assurance that you will, in due time, receive what you request of him. I want you to picture the scene and take a hold of the prayer that was said. A man is dead and has been buried for four days. His sisters and all his friends are gathered together mourning his death. They are, in some ways, putting the blame on Jesus because they knew he could have healed the man when he was sick; but because he delayed in coming, the man grew worse and eventually died.

If a member of your family had died, do you believe that there is someone with the anointing and power of God to raise that person from the dead? This may seem as a difficult question to answer but for some of the people who lived in the time of Jesus' ministry, the answer would be 'yes.' Listen to what Martha, the sister of the dead man said to Jesus. *"Lord, if thou hadst been here, my brother had not died. But I know, that even now, whatsoever thou wilt ask of God, God will give it thee."* Martha believed that whatever Jesus asked of God, it would be granted. Martha never specified that those things must be according to the will of God because she took it for granted that Jesus would ask only those things that were according to the will of God.

The Apostle John however underscored that requirement in 1 John 5:14-15. We ask according to the will of God when the Holy Spirit intercedes on our behalf. Romans 8:26 says, *"Likewise the Spirit also helpeth our infirmities: for we know not what we should pray for as we ought: but the Spirit itself maketh intercession for us with groanings which cannot be uttered.*

27 And he that searcheth the hearts knoweth what is the mind of the Spirit, because he maketh intercession for the saints according to the will of God."

So Jesus is now standing before the tomb which houses the dead man; and he is about to say a prayer concerning the situation. This is what the writer of the gospel said:

John 11:38-44:

"38 Jesus therefore again groaning in himself cometh to the grave. It was a cave, and a stone lay upon it.

39 Jesus said, Take ye away the stone. Martha, the sister of him that was dead, saith unto him, Lord, by this time he stinketh: for he hath been dead four days.

40 Jesus saith unto her, Said I not unto thee, that, if thou wouldest believe, thou shouldest see the glory of God?

*41 Then they took away the stone from the place where the dead was laid. And Jesus lifted up his eyes, and said, **Father, I thank thee that thou hast heard me.***

⁴²And I knew that thou hearest me always: but because of the people which stand by I said it, that they may believe that thou hast sent me.

⁴³And when he thus had spoken, he cried with a loud voice, Lazarus, come forth.

⁴⁴And he that was dead came forth, bound hand and foot with graveclothes: and his face was bound about with a napkin. Jesus saith unto them, Loose him, and let him go."

Jesus did not have to pray in order to perform the miracle because it was the Father in him who did the work. In John 14:10-11 Jesus said, "*Believest thou not that I am in the Father, and the Father in me? The words that I speak unto you I speak not of myself: but the Father that dwelleth in me, he doeth the works.*

¹¹Believe me that I am in the Father and the Father in me: or else believe me for the very works' sake."

Again, in John 5:19, he said, "*Verily, verily, I say unto you, The Son can do nothing of himself, but what he seeth the Father do: for what things soever he doeth, these also doeth the Son likewise."*

What can we learn from this incident than could be beneficial to the way we conduct our prayers? One thing for certain is that our prayers must bring glory to the Lord Jesus Christ. Our prayers must also be faith-filled that they may cause the hearers to be encouraged and have a renewed sense of trust in the promises of God. Ephesians 4:29 says, "*Let no corrupt communication proceed out of your mouth, but that which is good to the use of edifying, that it may minister grace unto the hearers.*" When Jesus prayed at the grave of Lazarus, it ministered grace, hope and the truth to those who were present; and that was the purpose of his prayer.

Notes

Luke 22:39-46

Mark 14:32-42

Prayer concerning his crucifixion:

Anyone who spent time with Jesus knew what great importance he placed on communicating with God through prayer. When we read the gospels, we realize how trustworthy this saying is. For example, Luke 5:16 says, *"So He himself often withdrew into the wilderness and prayed."* The writer, Luke tells of another occasion when Jesus set himself apart to pray. Luke 6:12 says, *"Now it came to pass in those days that He went out to the mountain to pray, and continued all night in prayer to God"* After having witnessed the intimacy that Jesus shared with the Father, it only seemed compelling that the disciples would ask him to teach them to pray (Luke 11:2); but not every prayer that Jesus said was appropriate for the disciples to say. For example, in Luke 22:39-46 there is a prayer that only Jesus could have said because it pertained to his crucifixion and death on a cross for the sin of the world.

The passage is listed here for convenience:

[39]And he came out, and went, as he was wont, to the mount of Olives; and his disciples also followed him.

[40]And when he was at the place, he said unto them, Pray that ye enter not into temptation.

[41]And he was withdrawn from them about a stone's cast, and kneeled down, and prayed,

[42]Saying, **Father, if thou be willing, remove this cup from me: nevertheless not my will, but thine, be done.**

[43]And there appeared an angel unto him from heaven, strengthening him.

[44]And being in an agony he prayed more earnestly: and his sweat was as it were great drops of blood falling down to the ground.

45And when he rose up from prayer, and was come to his disciples, he found them sleeping for sorrow,

46And said unto them, Why sleep ye? rise and pray, lest ye enter into temptation."

This simple prayer of Jesus has far more implications than what we observe in the written words. When we analyze this prayer, we recognize that Jesus was asking the Father to remove a cup from him. That was his desire but he quickly surrendered his desire in exchange for God's desire. The cup was representative of the New Testament. Mark 14:22-25 says, "*And as they did eat, Jesus took bread, and blessed, and brake it, and gave to them, and said, Take, eat: this is my body.*

*23And he took **the cup**, and when he had given thanks, he gave it to them: and they all drank of it.*

*24And he said unto them, **This is my blood of the new testament**, which is shed for many.*

25Verily I say unto you, I will drink no more of the fruit of the vine, until that day that I drink it new in the kingdom of God."

There are some who interpret this prayer as to mean that Jesus was asking the Father to cancel the mission of the cross but that is far from the truth. The mission could not be canceled because it had already taken place even before the foundation of the world. Revelation 13:8 says, "*And all that dwell upon the earth shall worship him, whose names are not written in the book of life of the Lamb slain from the foundation of the world."*

Jesus himself said in John 10:17-18, "*Therefore doth my Father love me, because I lay down my life, that I might take it again.*

18No man taketh it from me, but I lay it down of myself. I have power to lay it down, and I have power to take it again. This commandment have I received of my Father."

In John 15:13-14, he comforted his disciples saying, "*Greater love hath no man than this, that a man lay down his life for his friends.*

[14]Ye are my friends, if ye do whatsoever I command you."

In Matthew 17:22-23, he spoke plainly of his death, saying, *"The Son of man shall be betrayed into the hands of men:*

[23]And they shall kill him, and the third day he shall be raised again."

During the early part of his ministry, Jesus made an open statement which is recorded in John 3:16: *"For God so loved the world that he gave his only begotten Son, that whosoever believeth in him should not perish, but have everlasting life."*

The prophet Isaiah spoke of his death; Isaiah Chapter 53. John the Baptist addressed him as '**the Lamb of God that taketh away the sin of the world.**' (John 1:29)

Jesus also had determined that he must die for the sin of the world, and the decision could not be changed or altered. This what about Salvation which cannot be changed, altered or performed by anyone else but Jesus. Acts 4:12 says, *"Neither is there salvation in any other: for there is none other name under heaven given among men, whereby we must be saved."*

The petition that Jesus made was about the separation he would endure when he became the sacrificial lamb for the sin of the world. Romans 6:23 says, *"The wages of sin is death."* That death is separation from God and Jesus was the only one who could reunite sinful man with God the Father. In John 14:6, he said to his disciples, *"I am the Way, the Truth and the Life, no one can come to the Father except by me."* Jesus was prepared to die but the separation from the Father carried the greater pain.

We must be thankful at all times for the sacrifice that Jesus made on our behalf. When we pray to the Father, we must also relinquish our will and allow God's will to be done in our lives. Sin can no longer separate us from God because Jesus paid the price. 1 Peter 2:24 says, *"Who his own self bare our sins in his own body on the tree, that we, being dead to sins, should live unto righteousness: by whose stripes ye were healed."* We can however withdraw ourselves from him; for this reason, the Apostle James urges us with the statement, *"Draw nigh to God, and he will draw nigh to you;"* (James 4:8)

When we pray, 'Thy will be done,' we are asking God to be Lord of our lives and inviting him to express himself in which ever way he chooses that he alone may be glorified by it. The glory belongs to the Lord. Revelation 4:11 says, *"Thou art worthy, O Lord, to receive glory and honour and power: for thou hast created all things, and for thy pleasure they are and were created."*

I pray that God will open a door of opportunity for you that his will may be perform in your life.
I ask this in Jesus' name.
Amen.

Notes

PRAYER AND AUTHORITY

In the Name of Jesus

John 14:13-14; 16:23-24
Acts 4:30-31
Mark 16:17-20

John 14:13-14; 16:23-24

Prayer and authority bring with them a tremendous amount of power, but the true power lies in the source of that authority and in whose name we pray. In John Chapters 14 to 16, which may be classified as Jesus' farewell speech to his disciples, he made some profound statements as to how we should pray. In Luke Chapter 10, he also made a startling statement regarding power which would be observed throughout the New Testament. This power comes from the Greek word '*exousia*' which means '*authority*' and should not be confused with the word '*dunamis*' which also means 'power' but in the sense of strength.

There are two separate topics in this segment, but because they are interrelated we cannot talk about one without mentioning the other. In the gospel of John, Jesus gave the disciples the assurance that *if they were to ask anything in his name, he would do it* (**John 14:14**). Again in **John 16:23,** he took '*the asking*' one step further by introducing the Father as the one to whom we should directly our requests. This is what he said, *"And in that day ye shall ask me nothing. Verily, verily, I say unto you, Whatsoever ye shall ask the Father in my name, he will give it you."* If we examine those two scriptures, we will notice that in the first instance John 14:14, the result of the asking culminates in a **doing**; but in the second scripture John 16:23, the end result is a **giving**.

What are we to learn from these statements as it pertains to our prayers and our authority in a natural and spiritual arena? Before we attempt to answer this and other questions that may evolve from these statements, allow me to add another passage of scripture; John 16:24, "Hitherto have ye asked nothing in my name: ask, and ye shall receive, that your joy may be full." This statement is so typical of a good father. A good father always wants to see his children full of joy and so he invites them to ask for their desires.

I remember as a young lad, my father telling me to ask him for whatever I needed and he would give it to me. He would also encourage me to ask him for whatever I wanted him to do for me; and he promised he would do it. I said that to highlight what Jesus said in John 14:14. When we ask in Jesus' name, he will **perform**; but when we ask the Father, in Jesus' name, the Father will **give** it. The mysterious question remains; 'who do we ask, in Jesus' name that it would please Jesus to do it? Do we ask Jesus in his name, or do we simply voice our request in Jesus' name and he will do it?

Consider what I am about to say; ponder on it and then form your opinion. When Jesus said "ask anything in my name," he was not trying to change the peoples' way of praying, but instead, he was adding his name as an assurance that their prayers would be answered. People normally pray to God and that was acceptable even in the eyes of Jesus; but he was teaching them a new way which he was it. So when they prayed, they could ask for what they wanted, in his name. When they used his name, they were acknowledging that he is the way to the Father. In John 14:6, he said, "*I am the Way, the Truth and the Life; no one can come to the Father except by me.*"

Let us put this prayer into action so as to get a better understanding of the use of the name of Jesus, while in his presence.

Prayer addressed to Jesus

Lord Jesus,

I bow my knees before you, and confess that you are Lord to the glory of God the Father. I come to seek mercy and find grace to help in time of need. As you have forgiven me, so also have I forgiven those who have trespassed against me.

With a humble heart and a contrite spirit, I plead for the souls of those who have heard your word and are reluctant to be drawn to you.

I pray that you would cover me with your anointing that I may minister grace to them and cause them to be drawn closer to you.

Lord Jesus, I make this request knowing that you hear me; and because I know that you hear me, I believe that I shall have this petition.

I pray for peace, not only in my life but in the lives of all your people.

I pray for the peace of Jerusalem and your speedy return.

I ask this in your mighty, precious name.

In the name of Jesus;

Amen.

We must keep in mind that Jesus is not 'in a box' to be called upon at our convenience, and prayer is reaching out to him in a heartfelt manner. If we called upon Jesus for a need and invoked his name, would he not answer? What would cause him not to answer our prayers? Is it the fact that we called on him, in the authority of his name? It may sound foolish to us, but to him, it is a call for help and he will never turn us away. John 6:37 Jesus said, *"All that the Father giveth me shall come to me; and him that cometh to me I will in no wise cast out."* Acts 2:21 says, *"And it shall come to pass, that whosoever shall call on the name of the Lord shall be saved."*

Here is a prayer using the name of Jesus to request power and boldness for the work of the Kingdom of God. Acts 4:23-31 says;

²³And being let go, they went to their own company, and reported all that the chief priests and elders had said unto them.

²⁴And when they heard that, they lifted up their voice to God with one accord, and said, Lord, thou art God, which hast made heaven, and earth, and the sea, and all that in them is:

²⁵Who by the mouth of thy servant David hast said, Why did the heathen rage, and the people imagine vain things?

²⁶The kings of the earth stood up, and the rulers were gathered together against the Lord, and against his Christ.

*²⁷For of a truth against **thy holy child Jesus,** whom thou hast anointed, both Herod, and Pontius Pilate, with the Gentiles, and the people of Israel, were gathered together,*

²⁸For to do whatsoever thy hand and thy counsel determined before to be done.

²⁹And now, Lord, behold their threatenings: and grant unto thy servants, that with all boldness they may speak thy word,

*³⁰By stretching forth thine hand to heal; and that signs and wonders may be done **by the name of thy holy child Jesus.***

31And when they had prayed, the place was shaken where they were assembled together; and they were all filled with the Holy Ghost, and they spake the word of God with boldness.

This prayer was offered up that signs and wonders may be done **by the name of the holy child Jesus.** Should we get technical and say that Jesus was no longer a child and therefore the Apostles should not have referred to him as a child? Did God answer the prayer? Yes! He did and they were all filled with the Holy Ghost and began to speak the word of God with boldness. We cannot and should not try to limit to work and power of God.

Here is another simple prayer; and I say prayer because Jesus is involved. The moment we call upon the name of the Lord, we are no longer operating horizontally but vertically. We are at that point in time, reaching out to God and getting him involved in the situation because he is the healer and the supplier of our need. Exodus 15:26 says, *"I am the LORD that healeth thee."* Philippians 4:19 says, *"But my God shall supply all your need according to his riches in glory by Christ Jesus."*

Acts 3:6 is the request but the story begins at verse 1 and ends at verse 8. Here is the account:

1Now Peter and John went up together into the temple at the hour of prayer, being the ninth hour.

2And a certain man lame from his mother's womb was carried, whom they laid daily at the gate of the temple which is called Beautiful, to ask alms of them that entered into the temple;

3Who seeing Peter and John about to go into the temple asked an alms.

4And Peter, fastening his eyes upon him with John, said, Look on us.

5And he gave heed unto them, expecting to receive something of them.

6Then Peter said, Silver and gold have I none; but such as I have give I thee: **In the name of Jesus Christ of Nazareth** *rise up and walk.*

⁷And he took him by the right hand, and lifted him up: and immediately his feet and ankle bones received strength.

⁸And he leaping up stood, and walked, and entered with them into the temple, walking, and leaping, and praising God.

When we use the name of Jesus, we can accomplish great and mighty things; but we must believe on him and abide in him for them to be a reality. In John 14:12 Jesus said to his disciples, *"Verily, verily, I say unto you, He that believeth on me, the works that I do shall he do also; and greater works than these shall he do; because I go unto my Father."* In John 15:5, he used an allegory to describe himself as the true vine and said, *"I am the vine, ye are the branches: He that abideth in me, and I in him, the same bringeth forth much fruit: for without me ye can do nothing."*

The use of the name of Jesus is not for everyone but for those who have entrusted their lives to him; those who have accepted his death as the penalty for their sins. There is a story in the book of Acts that speaks clearly of this privilege. Acts 19:11-20 the physician Luke gave this account:

¹¹And God wrought special miracles by the hands of Paul:

¹²So that from his body were brought unto the sick handkerchiefs or aprons, and the diseases departed from them, and the evil spirits went out of them.

¹³Then certain of the vagabond Jews, exorcists, took upon them to call over them which had evil spirits the name of the LORD Jesus, saying, **We adjure you by Jesus whom Paul preacheth.**

¹⁴And there were seven sons of one Sceva, a Jew, and chief of the priests, which did so.

*¹⁵**And the evil spirit answered and said, Jesus I know, and Paul I know; but who are ye?***

¹⁶And the man in whom the evil spirit was leaped on them, and overcame them, and prevailed against them, so that they fled out of that house naked and wounded.

¹⁷And this was known to all the Jews and Greeks also dwelling at Ephesus; and fear fell on them all, and the name of the Lord Jesus was magnified.

¹⁸And many that believed came, and confessed, and shewed their deeds.

¹⁹Many of them also which used curious arts brought their books together, and burned them before all men: and they counted the price of them, and found it fifty thousand pieces of silver.

²⁰So mightily grew the word of God and prevailed.

Again we need to recognize the power that is offered by the use of the name of Jesus. This power is available to anyone who would believe in Jesus Christ and accept him as Lord and Saviour. This power will be manifested not only in their works but also in their prayers.

Mark 16:17-20 says, *"And these signs shall follow them that believe; In my name shall they cast out devils; they shall speak with new tongues;*

¹⁸They shall take up serpents; and if they drink any deadly thing, it shall not hurt them; they shall lay hands on the sick, and they shall recover."

¹⁹So then after the Lord had spoken unto them, he was received up into heaven, and sat on the right hand of God.

²⁰And they went forth, and preached every where, the Lord working with them, and confirming the word with signs following. Amen.

Prayer addressed to the Father

Father in Heaven,

I bow my knees before you, and confess my sins_____.
I seek your mercy and forgiveness; and I ask you to cleanse me from all unrighteousness. With a humble heart and a contrite spirit, I plead for the souls of those who have offended you through their ignorance and unbelief. I pray that you would draw them to your Son Jesus Christ that they may be saved.

I pray that you would cover me with your anointing that I may minister grace to anyone that you would put in my path.

Lord, I make this request knowing that you hear me; and because I know that you hear me, I believe that I shall have this petition.

I pray for peace, love, and the continued joy of your salvation; not only in my life but in the lives of all your people.

I ask this in the name of Jesus.

And I give him all the praise and all the glory.

Amen

In the next chapter, we will look at some of the prayers that were presented by the Apostle Paul and James, the half-brother of Jesus.

Notes

CHAPTER FIVE

The Prayer of the Apostle Paul

THE PRAYER OF PAUL

When we search the New Testament for prayers offered up by the Apostle Paul, we most often find passages indicating that he prayed; for himself, the church or both. For example, in **Romans 1:8-12**, he addressed the church at Rome with a message of thanksgiving, and a prayer expressing his desire to come and fellowship with them. He said, *"First, I thank my God through Jesus Christ for you all, that your faith is spoken of throughout the whole world.*

⁹For God is my witness, whom I serve with my spirit in the gospel of his Son, that without ceasing I make mention of you always in my prayers;

¹⁰Making request, if by any means now at length I might have a prosperous journey by the will of God to come unto you.

¹¹For I long to see you, that I may impart unto you some spiritual gift, to the end ye may be established;

¹²That is that I may be comforted together with you by the mutual faith both of you and me."

The Apostle Paul continued this form of greeting, thanksgiving and prayer throughout the New Testament; from the book of Romans to the book of Philemon. He never ceased to thank the Lord for the believers and for the faith they expressed in the Lord Jesus Christ. This is his prayer of thanksgiving for the saints at Corinth as documented in 1 Corinthians 1:1-9, *"Paul called to be an apostle of Jesus Christ through the will of God, and Sosthenes our brother,*

²Unto the church of God which is at Corinth, to them that are sanctified in Christ Jesus, called to be saints, with all that in every place call upon the name of Jesus Christ our Lord, both their's and our's:

³Grace be unto you, and peace, from God our Father, and from the Lord Jesus Christ.

⁴I thank my God always on your behalf, for the grace of God which is given you by Jesus Christ;

⁵That in every thing ye are enriched by him, in all utterance, and in all knowledge;

⁶Even as the testimony of Christ was confirmed in you:

⁷So that ye come behind in no gift; waiting for the coming of our Lord Jesus Christ:

⁸Who shall also confirm you unto the end, that ye may be blameless in the day of our Lord Jesus Christ.

⁹God is faithful, by whom ye were called unto the fellowship of his Son Jesus Christ our Lord."

We know that Paul did pray earnestly to the Lord because Jesus testified to it. In Acts 9:11-12, he spoke to a disciple named Ananias saying, *"Arise, and go into the street which is called Straight, and enquire in the house of Judas for one called Saul, of Tarsus: for, behold, he prayeth,*

¹²And hath seen in a vision a man named Ananias coming in, and putting his hand on him, that he might receive his sight."

So there is no doubt in our minds that Paul was a praying person. In every letter to the churches, he would pronounce a blessing upon them, and encourage them to hold fast to what they have learned from him concerning Jesus Christ.

To the Galatians, he said:

³"Grace be to you and peace from God the Father, and from our Lord Jesus Christ,

⁴Who gave himself for our sins, that he might deliver us from this present evil world, according to the will of God and our Father:

⁵To whom be glory for ever and ever. Amen." (Galatians 1:3-5)

To the Ephesians, he prayed for spiritual understanding:

¹⁵Wherefore I also, after I heard of your faith in the Lord Jesus, and love unto all the saints,

¹⁶Cease not to give thanks for you, making mention of you in my prayers;

¹⁷That the God of our Lord Jesus Christ, the Father of glory, may give unto you the spirit of wisdom and revelation in the knowledge of him:

¹⁸The eyes of your understanding being enlightened; that ye may know what is the hope of his calling, and what the riches of the glory of his inheritance in the saints,

¹⁹And what is the exceeding greatness of his power to us-ward who believe, according to the working of his mighty power,

²⁰Which he wrought in Christ, when he raised him from the dead, and set him at his own right hand in the heavenly places,

²¹Far above all principality, and power, and might, and dominion, and every name that is named, not only in this world, but also in that which is to come:

²²And hath put all things under his feet, and gave him to be the head over all things to the church,

²³Which is his body, the fulness of him that filleth all in all." (Ephesians 1:15-23)

To the Philippians, he offered a prayer of thanksgiving that resonated deep down from within his soul. This was his prayer:

³"I thank my God upon every remembrance of you,

⁴Always in every prayer of mine for you all making request with joy,

⁵For your fellowship in the gospel from the first day until now;

⁶Being confident of this very thing, that he which hath begun a good work in you will perform it until the day of Jesus Christ:

⁷Even as it is meet for me to think this of you all, because I have you in my heart; inasmuch as both in my bonds, and in the defense and confirmation of the gospel, ye all are partakers of my grace.

⁸For God is my record, how greatly I long after you all in the bowels of Jesus Christ.

⁹And this I pray, that your love may abound yet more and more in knowledge and in all judgment;

¹⁰That ye may approve things that are excellent; that ye may be sincere and without offence till the day of Christ.

¹¹Being filled with the fruits of righteousness, which are by Jesus Christ, unto the glory and praise of God." (Philippians 1:3-11)

In order to fully appreciate the depth of Paul's feelings, it is necessary to list the complete passage of scripture which will become valuable to you as you ponder on the verses. Some of the verses can be incorporated in your own prayers as you stand in the gap for friends, relatives and members of the body of Christ. It would be profitable for you to memorize and internalize some of these verses. There is nothing more precious than the word of God in your heart; for the bible says in Matthew 12:34, "for out of the abundance of the heart the mouth speaketh."

To the Colossians, he continued with his salutation and thanksgiving as he did with the other churches, but he prayed for them to know God's will and to conduct their lives pleasing unto the Lord. This was his salutation, his thanksgiving and the prayer that followed:

²˙To the saints and faithful brethren in Christ which are at Colosse: Grace be unto you, and peace, from God our Father and the Lord Jesus Christ.

³We give thanks to God and the Father of our Lord Jesus Christ, praying always for you,

⁴Since we heard of your faith in Christ Jesus, and of the love which ye have to all the saints,

⁵For the hope which is laid up for you in heaven, whereof ye heard before in the word of the truth of the gospel;

⁶Which is come unto you, as it is in all the world; and bringeth forth fruit, as it doth also in you, since the day ye heard of it, and knew the grace of God in truth:

⁷As ye also learned of Epaphras our dear fellowservant, who is for you a faithful minister of Christ;

⁸Who also declared unto us your love in the Spirit.

⁹For this cause we also, since the day we heard it, do not cease to pray for you, and to desire that ye might be filled with the knowledge of his will in all wisdom and spiritual understanding;

¹⁰That ye might walk worthy of the Lord unto all pleasing, being fruitful in every good work, and increasing in the knowledge of God;

¹¹Strengthened with all might, according to his glorious power, unto all patience and longsuffering with joyfulness;

¹²Giving thanks unto the Father, which hath made us meet to be partakers of the inheritance of the saints in light:

¹³Who hath delivered us from the power of darkness, and hath translated us into the kingdom of his dear Son:

[14]In whom we have redemption through his blood, even the forgiveness of sins:"

Paul would continue this trend of salutation and thanksgiving, making mention of anything that he saw that was significant in the lives of the members of the church. He would always complement them and encourage them to continue in the faith, in spite of the troubles and opposition they faced.

To the Thessalonians, this was his salutation, his thanksgiving and the prayer that followed:

[2]"We give thanks to God always for you all, making mention of you in our prayers;

[3]Remembering without ceasing your work of faith, and labour of love, and patience of hope in our Lord Jesus Christ, in the sight of God and our Father;

[4]Knowing, brethren beloved, your election of God." (1 Thessalonians 1:2-4)

The Prayer

[11]"Now God himself and our Father, and our Lord Jesus Christ, direct our way unto you.

[12]And the Lord make you to increase and abound in love one toward another, and toward all men, even as we do toward you:

[13]To the end he may stablish your hearts unblameable in holiness before God, even our Father, at the coming of our Lord Jesus Christ with all his saints."

In another instance, Paul urged the Thessalonians to pray for him and his fellow workers and he concluded with a benediction.

To the Thessalonians, this was his prayer request:

[1]"Finally, brethren, pray for us, that the word of the Lord may have free course, and be glorified, even as it is with you:

[2]And that we may be delivered from unreasonable and wicked men: for all men have not faith.

³But the Lord is faithful, who shall stablish you, and keep you from evil.

⁴And we have confidence in the Lord touching you that ye both do and will do the things which we command you.

⁵And the Lord direct your hearts into the love of God, and into the patient waiting for Christ."

The Benediction:

¹⁶ *"Now the Lord of peace himself give you peace always by all means. The Lord be with you all.*

¹⁷ *The salutation of Paul with mine own hand, which is the token in every epistle: so I write.*

¹⁸ *The grace of our Lord Jesus Christ be with you all. Amen."*

To Timothy:

The Apostle Paul was extremely fond of a young man named Timothy, and he did everything within his powers to educate this young man that he would become an effective leader in the church. Paul would write to Timothy concerning matters of the church, and in his letter he would address him as follows: *"Unto Timothy, my own son in the faith: Grace, mercy and peace, from God our Father, and Jesus Christ our Lord."* (2 Timothy 1:2)

He would always remind him that a day would never go by without his praying for him. This is his prayer and the desire of his heart as expressed in his letter to Timothy.

3 *"I thank God, whom I serve from my forefathers with pure conscience, that without ceasing I have remembrance of thee in my prayers night and day;*

⁴ *Greatly desiring to see thee, being mindful of thy tears, that I may be filled with joy;"* (2 Timothy 1:3-4)

Paul loved to pray both with the understanding and with the spirit, but he exercised wisdom even when he prayed. In 1 Corinthians 14:18-19, he said, *"I thank my God, I speak with tongues more than ye all:*

[19]Yet in the church I had rather speak five words with my understanding, that by my voice I might teach others also, than ten thousand words in an unknown tongue." There are many things that we need to understand; one of which is that not all prayers are answered. There was a time when the Apostle Paul prayed about a situation that was troubling him. It was one of those things that never seem to go away, even after you have prayed. Paul described it as 'a thorn in the flesh.' The account is found in 2 Corinthians 12:2-10. The passage is listed here for convenience:

2 Corinthians 12:2-10

[2]I knew a man in Christ above fourteen years ago, (whether in the body, I cannot tell; or whether out of the body, I cannot tell: God knoweth;) such an one caught up to the third heaven.

[3]And I knew such a man, (whether in the body, or out of the body, I cannot tell: God knoweth;)

[4]How that he was caught up into paradise, and heard unspeakable words, which it is not lawful for a man to utter.

[5]Of such an one will I glory: yet of myself I will not glory, but in mine infirmities.

[6]For though I would desire to glory, I shall not be a fool; for I will say the truth: but now I forbear, lest any man should think of me above that which he seeth me to be, or that he heareth of me.

[7]And lest I should be exalted above measure through the abundance of the revelations, there was given to me a thorn in the flesh, the messenger of Satan to buffet me, lest I should be exalted above measure.

[8]For this thing I besought the Lord thrice, that it might depart from me.

[9]And he said unto me, My grace is sufficient for thee: for my strength is made perfect in weakness. Most gladly therefore will I rather glory in my infirmities, that the power of Christ may rest upon me.

¹⁰Therefore I take pleasure in infirmities, in reproaches, in necessities, in persecutions, in distresses for Christ's sake: for when I am weak, then am I strong.

In verse 7-8, he said, "And *lest I should be exalted above measure through the abundance of the revelations, there was given to me a thorn in the flesh, the messenger of Satan to buffet me, lest I should be exalted above measure.*

⁸For this thing I besought the Lord thrice, that it might depart from me."

It is important, as a Christian, to know that God does not answer all of our prayers. It is not because they were not offered in faith, or out of God's will; but because God has chosen to allow the situation persist that you may be either strengthened by it for the work of the Kingdom; or weakened by it that to demonstrate the sufficiency of God. Either way, God gets the glory.

Paul prayed three times, asking the Lord to remove the obstacle; but his prayers were not answered. But God is gracious and will always comfort us in a way that we could understand the reason for his decisions. He would talk to us in our spirit by the Holy Spirit, and give us the power that we may overcome the obstacles that are set before us. In Paul's situation, this is what the Lord said: *"My grace is sufficient for thee; for my strength is made perfect in weakness."* (2 Corinthians 12:9)

The Apostle ended his second letter to the Corinthians with a blessing which is practiced in most churches today. He ended with these words; *"The grace of our Lord Jesus Christ, and the love of God, and the communion of the Holy Ghost be with you all. Amen."* (2 Corinthians 12:14)

To Titus

In Paul's two final letters he speaks about his sons in the faith, namely Titus and Onesimus. In his letter to Titus, he addressed him in the usual manner. In Titus 1:4, he said, *"To Titus, mine own son after the common faith: Grace, mercy, and peace, from God the Father and the Lord Jesus Christ our Saviour."* He gave him certain instructions and then he closed the letter with the benediction which is a prayer for blessing. The definition of 'benediction' is **'a prayer asking for God's blessing, usually at the end of a Christian service.'**

To Philemon with an appeal for Onesimus:

In this letter, the Apostle Paul is appealing for the freedom and liberty of another son whom he had begotten in the faith. In verse 10, he urged Philemon, saying, "*I beseech thee for my son Onesimus, whom I have begotten in my bonds.*" Onesimus was a runaway slave who became a Christian through the preaching of the Apostle Paul who loved him as a son. Hoping to seek his freedom as a man who could serve his master, not as a slave but as a brother in Christ; Paul wrote a letter to Philemon and addressed the matter. He challenged him with these words which are recorded in verse 17-21:

17 "If thou count me therefore a partner, receive him as myself.

18 If he hath wronged thee, or oweth thee ought, put that on mine account;

19 I Paul have written it with mine own hand, I will repay it: albeit I do not say to thee how thou owest unto me even thine own self besides.

20 Yea, brother, let me have joy of thee in the Lord: refresh my bowels in the Lord.

21 Having confidence in thy obedience I wrote unto thee, knowing that thou wilt also do more than I say."

Then Paul made a remarkable statement which would trigger Philemon to pray for him; that his prayers would open a way for Paul to visit him. So not only did the Apostle Paul pray for the saints, he also encouraged then to pray for him. And as usual he ended his letter with the benediction. Verse 25 says, "The grace of our Lord Jesus Christ be with your spirit. Amen"

It is my prayer that you would carefully consider what the Apostle Paul has said in his letters to the churches and the individuals; and let it be your prayers also.

I pray in Jesus' name. Amen.

Notes

CHAPTER SIX

Prayer and Fasting

PRAYER AND FASTING

We use the term 'prayer and fasting' perhaps as a constant reminder that one can pray without fasting; but should not fast without praying. When a person enters into a fast, he or she has determined to deprive him or herself from the basic necessities for sustaining life; and trusting the Lord to sustain them during that period of time. It is at that time that one can become very susceptible to temptations. Jesus told his disciples to pray lest they enter into temptation (Luke 22:46). A perfect example of what could happen when a person enters a fast is found in the gospel of Matthew, Chapter 4, verses 1-11.

The passage is listed here for convenience:

¹Then was Jesus led up of the Spirit into the wilderness to be tempted of the devil.

²And when he had fasted forty days and forty nights, he was afterward an hungred.

³And when the tempter came to him, he said, If thou be the Son of God, **command that these stones be made bread.**

⁴But he answered and said, It is written, Man shall not live by bread alone, but by every word that proceedeth out of the mouth of God.

⁵Then the devil taketh him up into the holy city, and setteth him on a pinnacle of the temple,

*⁶And saith unto him, If thou be the Son of God, **cast thyself down:** for it is written, He shall give his angels charge concerning thee: and in their hands they shall bear thee up, lest at any time thou dash thy foot against a stone.*

⁷Jesus said unto him, It is written again, Thou shalt not tempt the Lord thy God.

⁸Again, the devil taketh him up into an exceeding high mountain, and sheweth him all the kingdoms of the world, and the glory of them;

*⁹And saith unto him, **All these things will I give thee, if thou wilt fall down and worship me.***

¹⁰Then saith Jesus unto him, Get thee hence, Satan: for it is written, Thou shalt worship the Lord thy God, and him only shalt thou serve.

¹¹Then the devil leaveth him, and, behold, angels came and ministered unto him.

In this passage, we observe three distinct temptations though there may have been many more that were not mentioned. The devil knew in what area he should focus his temptations. He knew that Jesus was hungry after fasting for forty days and forty nights and since there was no food in the wilderness, he presented the solution to the hunger problem; *'change these stones to bread.'* The devil will always attack you at your weakest point. Whatever you crave in life, will become an open door for the devil to attack you and try to cause you to sin. This is one of the reasons why addictions most often lead to all sorts of crimes against humanity. There is an addiction for power; for food; for sex; for drugs and the like. There are also those who deprive themselves of the basic necessities of life, such as food, in order to conform themselves to certain worldly standards. This also opens a door for the devil to take control of their lives since they are now at their weakest point. A good example is the woman who wants to become a model, and so she deprives herself of food in order to attain a certain weight which under normal circumstances would be detrimental to her health.

Jesus understood how important it was to have the word of God present, not only when you fast but at all times. He knew that prayer must be at the center of all your activities. The bible says in Ephesians 5:18, *"Praying always with all prayer and supplication in the Spirit, and watching thereunto with all perseverance and supplication for all saints;"*

1 Thessalonians 5:17 says, *"Pray without ceasing."*

Fasting without prayer is merely abstinence from food for personal reasons; but when prayer is included, God becomes a part of the process.

There is a danger that is always lurking when people are fasting. Their weaknesses are exposed; and where God can be instrumental in providing strength, the devil also seeks to magnify your weakness. 1 Corinthians 7:5 says, *"Defraud ye not one the other, except it be with consent for a time, that ye may give yourselves to fasting and prayer; and come together again, that Satan tempt you not for your incontinency."* If you have a sex addiction, he will encourage you to go and seek a relationship that would fulfill that addiction. If you are suicidal, he will show you ways to commit suicide. One should never give way to the devil. Any thought that is not of God should be cast down and brought to the obedience of Christ (2 Corinthians 10:4-5). When Jesus was tempted concerning his hunger, he quoted the word of God. We also must follow that example and quote the word of God when we are faced with temptation. This brings up a very important point which is the knowledge of God's word. It is therefore an obligation for every believer to study and internalize God's word as their weapon of defense against the evil one.

We need to put on the full armor of God that we may be able to stand up against the wiles of the devil. Listen to what the Apostle Paul said to the Ephesians as recorded in Ephesians 6:10-18:

10Finally, my brethren, be strong in the Lord, and in the power of his might.

11Put on the whole armour of God, that ye may be able to stand against the wiles of the devil.

12For we wrestle not against flesh and blood, but against principalities, against powers, against the rulers of the darkness of this world, against spiritual wickedness in high places.

13Wherefore take unto you the whole armour of God, that ye may be able to withstand in the evil day, and having done all, to stand.

14Stand therefore, having your loins girt about with truth, and having on the breastplate of righteousness;

¹⁵And your feet shod with the preparation of the gospel of peace;

¹⁶Above all, taking the shield of faith, wherewith ye shall be able to quench all the fiery darts of the wicked.

¹⁷And take the helmet of salvation, and the sword of the Spirit, which is the word of God:

¹⁸Praying always with all prayer and supplication in the Spirit, and watching thereunto with all perseverance and supplication for all saints;

When we enter into a fast, we must be equipped to face the temptations that will follow. Temptations will come, but since we are children of God, we can be assured that he will not leave us unattended. 1 Corinthians 10:13 says, *"There hath no temptation taken you but such as is common to man: but God is faithful, who will not suffer you to be tempted above that ye are able; but will with the temptation also make a way to escape, that ye may be able to bear it."*

How and why we fast:

What happens when we fast is clear; there is temptation but there is also a spiritual connection with God, and as in the case of Jesus, consolation from heavenly hosts (Matthew 4:11). How and why we fast must also be taken into consideration because it can also be offensive to God and the results may not turn out the way you expect. Let us look at two instances of fasting and see what effect they had on the Lord. The first example is taken from the book of **Jonah; Chapter 3**, **verses 1-10** and the second is from **2 Samuel, Chapter 12**, **verses 1-24**

Jonah, Chapter 3:1-10 The passage is listed here for convenience:

¹And the word of the LORD came unto Jonah the second time, saying,

²Arise, go unto Nineveh, that great city, and preach unto it the preaching that I bid thee.

³So Jonah arose, and went unto Nineveh, according to the word of the LORD. Now Nineveh was an exceeding great city of three days' journey.

⁴And Jonah began to enter into the city a day's journey, and he cried, and said, Yet forty days, and Nineveh shall be overthrown.

⁵So the people of Nineveh believed God, and proclaimed a fast, and put on sackcloth, from the greatest of them even to the least of them.

⁶For word came unto the king of Nineveh, and he arose from his throne, and he laid his robe from him, and covered him with sackcloth, and sat in ashes.

⁷And he caused it to be proclaimed and published through Nineveh by the decree of the king and his nobles, saying, Let neither man nor beast, herd nor flock, taste any thing: let them not feed, nor drink water:

⁸But let man and beast be covered with sackcloth, and cry mightily unto God: yea, let them turn every one from his evil way, and from the violence that is in their hands.

⁹Who can tell if God will turn and repent, and turn away from his fierce anger, that we perish not?

¹⁰And God saw their works, that they turned from their evil way; and God repented of the evil, that he had said that he would do unto them; and he did it not.

Verse 4 tells the reason why they fasted.
Verses 6-8 describe how they performed the fast.
Verse 10 shows the result of the fast.

The people of Nineveh fasted because they believed the message that the Prophet Jonah preached to them; that their city would be overthrown within forty days. They did not carry out the fast simply because of what Jonah said but because they believed God. If they did not believe that it was God speaking through the Prophet, they would not have fasted. So whenever someone prophesizes, it is of great importance and an obligation on the part of the hearer to test the spirit to see if it is of God. 1 John 4:1-3 says, *"¹Beloved, believe not every spirit, but try the spirits whether they are of God: because many false prophets are gone out into the world.*

²Hereby know ye the Spirit of God: Every spirit that confesseth that Jesus Christ is come in the flesh is of God:

³And every spirit that confesseth not that Jesus Christ is come in the flesh is not of God: and this is that spirit of antichrist, whereof ye have heard that it should come; and even now already is it in the world."

One should never be too quick to believe everything he or she hears.

The people of Nineveh fasted in the traditional fashion by covering themselves with sackcloth. The king however did something very remarkable which demonstrated his humbleness before God. He disrobed himself of his kingly attire and became like the rest of the people. He demonstrated that when we come before the Lord, no one should consider himself to be greater than the other. Romans 3:10 and 23 says, *"there is none righteous; no, not one; for all have sinned and come short of the glory of God."* The king knew that there was a king that was far superior than he was. That king is known to us as Jesus Christ whom the bible describes in the book of Revelation as the King of kings and the Lord of lords (Revelation 19:16).

The people of Nineveh fasted and received a just reward. They humbled themselves and prayed and turned from their evil ways and their violence, and were able to obtain mercy from God. 2 Chronicles 7:14 says, *"If my people, which are called by my name, shall humble themselves, and pray, and seek my face, and turn from their wicked ways; then will I hear from heaven, and will forgive their sin, and will heal their land."*

Jonah 3:10 says, *"And God saw their works, that they turned from their evil way; and God repented of the evil, that he had said that he would do unto them; and he did it not."*

The people of Nineveh fasted because there was impending danger upon their city; and this is the attitude of many Christians. They fast and pray only when there is impending danger in their midst. Jesus alluded to this when he spoke to his disciples at the bottom of the mountain. They were unable to heal a demoniac boy and could not understand why it seemed that they did not have the power to perform the miracle. Jesus rebuked the devil and the child was cured from that very hour. Then the disciples took Jesus aside and asked him why they were unable to cast out the devil. Jesus gave them a twofold answer which can be applied to many of us today. He said, *"Because of your unbelief: for verily I say unto you, If ye have faith as a grain of mustard seed, ye shall say unto this mountain, Remove hence to yonder place; and it shall remove; and nothing shall be impossible unto you.*

[21]Howbeit this kind goeth not out but by prayer and fasting." (Matthew 17:20-21).

If we compare the people of Nineveh to the disciples, we recognize that there was no unbelief; they believed God. They also fasted and prayed, unlike the disciples who relied totally on the power that was entrusted to them to perform the miracles. While the total dependence on Jesus was necessary even compulsory, prayer and fasting was also a crucial part of the Christian life which the disciples neglected.

Let us always remember to devote some time to prayer and fasting, not only when the times are troubling, but especially when the times are good. We ought to be proactive in our approach to the Christian life. We are not here just to reap the benefits of seeds sown by others, but we also must sow seeds of love and peace, kindness and compassion which contribute to the type of fast that the Lord requires of us. Isaiah 58:6-12 says, *"Is not this the fast that I have chosen? to loose the bands of wickedness, to undo the heavy burdens, and to let the oppressed go free, and that ye break every yoke?*

[7]Is it not to deal thy bread to the hungry, and that thou bring the poor that are cast out to thy house? when thou seest the naked, that thou cover him; and that thou hide not thyself from thine own flesh?

[8]Then shall thy light break forth as the morning, and thine health shall spring forth speedily: and thy righteousness shall go before thee; the glory of the LORD shall be thy reward.

[9]Then shalt thou call, and the LORD shall answer; thou shalt cry, and he shall say, Here I am. If thou take away from the midst of thee the yoke, the putting forth of the finger, and speaking vanity;

[10]And if thou draw out thy soul to the hungry, and satisfy the afflicted soul; then shall thy light rise in obscurity, and thy darkness be as the noon day:

[11]And the LORD shall guide thee continually, and satisfy thy soul in drought, and make fat thy bones: and thou shalt be like a watered garden, and like a spring of water, whose waters fail not.

[12]And they that shall be of thee shall build the old waste places: thou shalt raise up the foundations of many generations; and thou shalt be called, The repairer of the breach, The restorer of paths to dwell in."

This is the type of fast that is most effective; a fast that is built around compassion for the poor and needy and anyone who is depressed or oppressed. In Matthew 25:3-, Jesus pointed out the importance of reaching out to those in need. He said, *"For I was an hungred, and ye gave me meat: I was thirsty, and ye gave me drink: I was a stranger, and ye took me in:*

[36]Naked, and ye clothed me: I was sick, and ye visited me: I was in prison, and ye came unto me.

[37]Then shall the righteous answer him, saying, Lord, when saw we thee an hungred, and fed thee? or thirsty, and gave thee drink?

[38]When saw we thee a stranger, and took thee in? or naked, and clothed thee?

[39]Or when saw we thee sick, or in prison, and came unto thee?

[40]And the King shall answer and say unto them, Verily I say unto you, Inasmuch as ye have done it unto one of the least of these my brethren, ye have done it unto me."

Prayer
We thank the Lord for his mercy and kindness and for the gift of his Son Jesus Christ who divested himself of all his glory (John 17:5) and became human like us to share in our suffering;

To die on a cross that we whosoever believe might have eternal life and be reunited with God.

Father, we thank you for your mercy and your kindness in the midst of these troubling times. We offer bodies a living sacrifice, washed in the blood of Christ that it may be holy and acceptable to you, O Lord.

Help us to exercise compassion and kindness to those in need.
Enable us to have the right motives when we fast that the results may be fruitful and pleasing to you.

We pray and offer our praises and petitions in the name of Jesus Christ, our Lord.
Amen.

Notes

Prayer and Fasting

2 Samuel, Chapter 12:1-24

This is the story of a man who had committed a sin that was unto death; the sin of adultery but he was forgiven by the Lord. However there are always consequences to sin and no type of fast is able to erase the stain of sin except the blood of Jesus Christ. This is an interesting story and must be told from the beginning of the chapter in order to truly observe the goodness, mercy and justice of the Lord. You will also observe the implementation of the principle that is taught in 1 Corinthians 7:5. which says, *"Defraud ye not one the other, except it be with consent for a time, that ye may give yourselves to fasting and prayer; and come together again, that Satan tempt you not for your incontinency."*

2 Samuel, Chapter 12:1-24

The passage is listed here for convenience:

¹And the LORD sent Nathan unto David. And he came unto him, and said unto him, There were two men in one city; the one rich, and the other poor.

²The rich man had exceeding many flocks and herds:

³But the poor man had nothing, save one little ewe lamb, which he had bought and nourished up: and it grew up together with him, and with his children; it did eat of his own meat, and drank of his own cup, and lay in his bosom, and was unto him as a daughter.

⁴And there came a traveller unto the rich man, and he spared to take of his own flock and of his own herd, to dress for the wayfaring man that was come unto him; but took the poor man's lamb, and dressed it for the man that was come to him.

⁵And David's anger was greatly kindled against the man; and he said to Nathan, As the LORD liveth, the man that hath done this thing shall surely die:

⁶And he shall restore the lamb fourfold, because he did this thing, and because he had no pity.

7And Nathan said to David, Thou art the man. Thus saith the LORD God of Israel, I anointed thee king over Israel, and I delivered thee out of the hand of Saul;

8And I gave thee thy master's house, and thy master's wives into thy bosom, and gave thee the house of Israel and of Judah; and if that had been too little, I would moreover have given unto thee such and such things.

9Wherefore hast thou despised the commandment of the LORD, to do evil in his sight? thou hast killed Uriah the Hittite with the sword, and hast taken his wife to be thy wife, and hast slain him with the sword of the children of Ammon.

10Now therefore the sword shall never depart from thine house; because thou hast despised me, and hast taken the wife of Uriah the Hittite to be thy wife.

11Thus saith the LORD, Behold, I will raise up evil against thee out of thine own house, and I will take thy wives before thine eyes, and give them unto thy neighbour, and he shall lie with thy wives in the sight of this sun.

12For thou didst it secretly: but I will do this thing before all Israel, and before the sun.

13And David said unto Nathan, I have sinned against the LORD. And Nathan said unto David, The LORD also hath put away thy sin; thou shalt not die.

14Howbeit, because by this deed thou hast given great occasion to the enemies of the LORD to blaspheme, the child also that is born unto thee shall surely die.

15And Nathan departed unto his house. And the LORD struck the child that Uriah's wife bare unto David, and it was very sick.

16David therefore besought God for the child; and David fasted, and went in, and lay all night upon the earth.

17And the elders of his house arose, and went to him, to raise him up from the earth: but he would not, neither did he eat bread with them.

¹⁸And it came to pass on the seventh day, that the child died. And the servants of David feared to tell him that the child was dead: for they said, Behold, while the child was yet alive, we spake unto him, and he would not hearken unto our voice: how will he then vex himself, if we tell him that the child is dead?

¹⁹But when David saw that his servants whispered, David perceived that the child was dead: therefore David said unto his servants, Is the child dead? And they said, He is dead.

²⁰Then David arose from the earth, and washed, and anointed himself, and changed his apparel, and came into the house of the LORD, and worshipped: then he came to his own house; and when he required, they set bread before him, and he did eat.

²¹Then said his servants unto him, What thing is this that thou hast done? thou didst fast and weep for the child, while it was alive; but when the child was dead, thou didst rise and eat bread.

²²And he said, While the child was yet alive, I fasted and wept: for I said, Who can tell whether GOD will be gracious to me, that the child may live?

²³But now he is dead, wherefore should I fast? can I bring him back again? I shall go to him, but he shall not return to me.

²⁴And David comforted Bathsheba his wife, and went in unto her, and lay with her: and she bare a son, and he called his name Solomon: and the LORD loved him.

Verses 14-15 tell the reason why they fasted.
Verse 16 describes how he performed the fast.
Verse 19 shows the result of the fast.
Verse 24 shows his obligation to his wife after the fast.

According to the text, God was displeased with the sin of adultery. He was then and will be even now. On the other hand, when David had relations with the same woman who eventually became his wife and bore him a child,

God loved the child. God is a God that loves to operate in covenant; and the covenant of marriage has always been very special to God. In Genesis 2:18, the Lord God said, *"It is not good that the man should be alone; I will make him a help meet for him."* Genesis 2:21-24 describes the operation that took place that gave way to the first wedding ceremony. This is what the bible says:

²¹And the LORD God caused a deep sleep to fall upon Adam, and he slept: and he took one of his ribs, and closed up the flesh instead thereof;

²²And the rib, which the LORD God had taken from man, made he a woman, and brought her unto the man.

²³And Adam said, This is now bone of my bones, and flesh of my flesh: she shall be called Woman, because she was taken out of Man.

²⁴Therefore shall a man leave his father and his mother, and shall cleave unto his wife: and they shall be one flesh.

The message is clear and simply: God hates sin and unless we repent, we will die in our sins. In a message to the Jews concerning unbelief, which in itself is a sin, he said, *"Ye are from beneath; I am from above: ye are of this world; I am not of this world.*

²⁴I said therefore unto you, that ye shall die in your sins: for if ye believe not that I am he, ye shall die in your sins." These Jews would not accept him as the Saviour of the world neither would they repent of their sins. Many of us today are harboring sin in our lives and are reluctant to come forward and confess them to the Lord. If we refuse to confess our sins, God still remains faithful and just but he cannot forgive them unless we confess them. We can choose to die in our sins, or we can confess them and be cleansed of all unrighteousness. The decision is ours.

In the story listed above, **David fasted because** he thought he could receive mercy from the Lord; that he would save the life of the child. It just seems natural that when people are in a bad situation and are helpless, they respond with humility. Some rely on prayer while others include fasting with prayer.

David fasted by lying on the earth all night for seven days, but it did not help his cause. The child eventually died as the Prophet Nathan had said. David did not allow the end result to get the better of him; rather he shook the dust off his clothes and kept his focus on the Lord with prayer and thanksgiving. The first thing he did when he ended his fast was in alignment with the teaching of 1 Corinthians 7:5. The text says, *"And David comforted Bathsheba his wife, and went in unto her, and lay with her: and she bare a son, and he called his name Solomon: and the LORD loved him* (2 Samuel 12:24).

God was pleased with the way David went about having this child. The Lord loved the child; not to say that he hated the other because God loves the children; as a matter of fact, God loves us all. John 3:16 says, *"For God so loved the world, that he gave his only begotten Son, that whosoever believeth in him should not perish, but have everlasting life."* The truth remains that the wages of sin is death; but the gift of God is eternal life through Jesus Christ our Lord.

When Jesus walked the earth, he was very critical of the way certain things were done especially when it pertained to prayer and fasting. Listen to what he said about fasting: Matthew 6:16-18 says, *"Moreover when ye fast, be not, as the hypocrites, of a sad countenance: for they disfigure their faces, that they may appear unto men to fast. Verily I say unto you, They have their reward.*

¹⁷But thou, when thou fastest, anoint thine head, and wash thy face;

¹⁸That thou appear not unto men to fast, but unto thy Father which is in secret: and thy Father, which seeth in secret, shall reward thee openly."

He was also critical about the way people offered their prayers. This is what he said in Matthew 6:5-8, *"And when thou prayest, thou shalt not be as the hypocrites are: for they love to pray standing in the synagogues and in the corners of the streets, that they may be seen of men. Verily I say unto you, They have their reward.*

⁶But thou, when thou prayest, enter into thy closet, and when thou hast shut thy door, pray to thy Father which is in secret; and thy Father which seeth in secret shall reward thee openly.

⁷But when ye pray, use not vain repetitions, as the heathen do: for they think that they shall be heard for their much speaking.

⁸Be not ye therefore like unto them: for your Father knoweth what things ye have need of, before ye ask him."

Since he thought that their way of praying was inadequate, he offered them a guideline to prayer which we call the Lord's Prayer. So Jesus said, *"After this manner therefore pray ye: Our Father which art in heaven, Hallowed be thy name.*

¹⁰Thy kingdom come, Thy will be done in earth, as it is in heaven.

¹¹Give us this day our daily bread.

¹²And forgive us our debts, as we forgive our debtors.

¹³And lead us not into temptation, but deliver us from evil: For thine is the kingdom, and the power, and the glory, for ever. Amen."

Notes

CHAPTER SEVEN

The Prayer of Jonah
The Prayer of Hannah
The Prayer of Solomon

THE PRAYER OF JONAH

The prayer of Jonah has to be one of the most extraordinary prayers in the bible. It was the only prayer that was offered up to God from the belly of a fish. There is significant because it has a direct reference to the death and burial of Jesus Christ.

In the gospel of Luke, chapter 11, verses 29-30, Jesus spoke about Jonah in the belly of the fish, saying, *"This is an evil generation: they seek a sign; and there shall no sign be given it, but the sign of Jonas the prophet.*

30 For as Jonas was a sign unto the Ninevites, so shall also the Son of man be to this generation."

Jonah's prayer was a prayer for deliverance; that was his desire in his time of trouble. When Jonah was swallowed up by the fish, he had a certain amount of time to decide if he should accept death or call upon the Lord for his salvation. He knew he was a sinner and in desperate need of a Saviour. Many of us today are in a similar situation yet some refuse to call upon the Lord. There is a reason why Jonah was able to call upon the Lord; and the reason is because he knew the Lord. Those that do not call upon the Lord are the ones that are still alienated from him. The Apostle Paul said in Romans 10:12-14, *"For there is no difference between the Jew and the Greek: for the same Lord over all is rich unto all that call upon him.*

13 For whosoever shall call upon the name of the Lord shall be saved.

14 How then shall they call on him in whom they have not believed? and how shall they believe in him of whom they have not heard? and how shall they hear without a preacher?"

As Christians who have trusted our lives in the Lord Jesus Christ we must never give up hope even in the worst of situations. But what about Jesus; how did he respond when he was in the belly of the earth? Jesus did not call out to the Father from the grave. He called out to him from the cross as he bore the sin of the world. The bible says in Matthew 27:46, *And about the ninth hour Jesus cried with a loud voice, saying, "Eli, Eli, lama sabachthani?" that is to say, My God, my God, why hast thou forsaken me?* He also called out to him in prayer, in the Garden of Gethsemane, as he struggled with the notion of being separated from the Father. Hebrews 5:7 says, *"Who in the days of his flesh, when he had offered up prayers and supplications with strong crying and tears unto him that was able to save him from death, and was heard in that he feared;"*

There are other interesting points about the prayer of Jonah that could be helpful to us when we pray for deliverance from threatening circumstances.

The prayer is listed here for convenience:

Jonah 2:1-10

¹Then Jonah prayed unto the LORD his God out of the fish's belly,

²And said, I cried by reason of mine affliction unto the LORD, and he heard me; out of the belly of hell cried I, and thou heardest my voice.

³For thou hadst cast me into the deep, in the midst of the seas; and the floods compassed me about: all thy billows and thy waves passed over me.

⁴Then I said, I am cast out of thy sight; yet I will look again toward thy holy temple.

⁵The waters compassed me about, even to the soul: the depth closed me round about, the weeds were wrapped about my head.

⁶I went down to the bottoms of the mountains; the earth with her bars was about me for ever: yet hast thou brought up my life from corruption, O LORD my God.

⁷When my soul fainted within me I remembered the LORD: and my prayer came in unto thee, into thine holy temple.

⁸They that observe lying vanities forsake their own mercy.

⁹But I will sacrifice unto thee with the voice of thanksgiving; I will pay that that I have vowed. Salvation is of the LORD. ¹⁰And the LORD spake unto the fish, and it vomited out Jonah upon the dry land.

First of all, we should know that Jonah was responsible for the perilous situation that was upon him. It was the direct result of disobedience to the directive that was given to him by the Lord. Because of the impending danger upon his life, he was prepared to make whatever sacrifice that was necessary to halt the process. Perhaps he understood then what it meant when the bible says, *"Obedience is better than sacrifice"* (1 Samuel 15:22). Jonah knew it was the Lord who had thrown him into the sea; and as dangerous as that was, he was more concerned about being separated from the Lord than loosing his own life. It was the same with Jesus when he prayed in the Garden of Gethsemane saying, *"Father, if thou be willing, remove this cup from me; nevertheless not my will, but thine, be done."* As Christians, we have the mind of Christ (1 Corinthians 2:16) and therefore we should think like him and allow the Father's will to be done in our lives.

Jonah ran from the Lord instead of toward the Lord and found himself in a place of desolation and solitude where only the grace of God could be of any effect. Therefore he cried out in desperation. There are many people today, both young and old who are caught up in situations that encompass them as the waters of the sea. Their minds have been distorted with the effect of weeds which are wrapped about their heads; even in their heads and they have lost a sense of direction. Like Jonah, they are running away from the Lord in a direction that that leads to disaster. When we find ourselves in such places, we must cry out in desperation; humbling ourselves under the mighty hand of God that he may exalt us in due time (1 Peter 5:6). We must draw near to God and he will draw near to us (James 4:8).

Jonah was pleading for his life. He was asking forgiveness and promising to offer himself a living sacrifice with the voice of thanksgiving. He knew that salvation was of the Lord and there was no alternative. No one else could save him from his situation but the Lord. **Acts 4:12** states, *"Neither is there salvation in any other: for there is none other name under heaven given among men, whereby we must be saved."* **Acts 2:21** says, *"And it shall come to pass, that whosoever shall call upon the name of the Lord shall be saved."* **Romans 10:9** promises, *"That if thou shalt confess with thy mouth the Lord Jesus, and shalt believe in thine heart that God hath raised him from the dead, thou shalt be saved".* **Mark 16:16** declares, *"He that believeth and is baptized shall be saved; but he that believeth not shall be damned."* Jonah believed, and it almost seemed as if he was baptized when he was cast into the sea. **Matthew 24:13** says, *"But he that shall endure unto the end, the same shall be saved."* Jonah did endure till the end, offering prayers for his deliverance and the Lord heard his cry.

When we pray for deliverance, we must empty ourselves of everything that is not of the Lord and *cast it upon him because he cares for us* (1 Peter 5:7)

Even as Jonah did, we must wait upon the Lord; believing that he has heard our prayers. According to 1 John 5:14-15, *this is the confidence that we have in him, that, if we ask any thing according to his will, he heareth us:*

¹⁵And if we know that he hear us, whatsoever we ask, we know that we have the petitions that we desired of him.

Jonah 2:10 says, *"And the Lord spake unto the fish, and it vomited out Jonah upon the dry land."* The fish in this story was more obedient to the Lord than Jonah was. Everything that has breath must obey the Lord; even the trees. For example, in Matthew 21:19 says, *"And when he (Jesus) saw a fig tree in the way, he came to it, and found nothing thereon, but leaves only, and said unto it, Let no fruit grow on thee henceforward for ever. And presently the fig tree withered away."*

Jonah was blessed because he received what he did not deserve; he received grace and mercy from the Lord. It is the grace of God that saves us. Ephesians 2:8-9 says, *"For by grace are ye saved through faith; and that not of yourselves: it is the gift of God:*

⁹Not of works, lest any man should boast." Jonah vowed to thank the Lord for what he had done; so also must we thank him for all the things he has done for us. **Psalms 105:1** says, *"O give thanks unto the LORD; call upon*

his name: make known his deeds among the people." **Psalms 107:1** reiterates the same message, *"O give thanks unto the LORD, for he is good: for his mercy endureth for ever."*

Let us give thanks unto the Lord. Let us praise him.

Psalms 150 declares:

[1]Praise ye the LORD. Praise God in his sanctuary: praise him in the firmament of his power.

[2]Praise him for his mighty acts: praise him according to his excellent greatness.

[3]Praise him with the sound of the trumpet: praise him with the psaltery and harp.

[4]Praise him with the timbrel and dance: praise him with stringed instruments and organs.

[5]Praise him upon the loud cymbals: praise him upon the high sounding cymbals.

[6]Let every thing that hath breath praise the LORD. Praise ye the LORD.

Amen.

Notes

THE PRAYER OF HANNAH

Hannah was one of the wives of a man named Elkanah, the other was Peninnah. This story is about Hannah and what she requested of the Lord in prayer. Hannah was barren while Peninnah was fertile and bore children for her husband. While people in the twenty-first century do not openly mock barren women, it was quite the opposite in earlier times. Hannah was mocked by her adversary. This went on for many years until Hannah became so despondent and frustrated over her own barrenness that she cried to the Lord of Host. (1 Samuel is the first book of the Old Testament to use the phrase "Lord of hosts.") She prayed an effectual, fervent prayer for the desire of her heart; and it was according to the will of God. In this story we will learn about the silent prayer; moving lips that produce no sound, yet God hears every word.

In order to appreciate the heart-felt prayers of Hannah, the passage is listed for convenience.

1 Samuel 1:1-18

¹Now there was a certain man of Ramathaimzophim, of mount Ephraim, and his name was Elkanah, the son of Jeroham, the son of Elihu, the son of Tohu, the son of Zuph, an Ephrathite:

*²And he had two wives; the name of the one was Hannah, and the name of the other Peninnah: and Peninnah had children, but **Hannah had no children.***

*³And this man went up out of his city yearly to worship and to sacrifice unto **the LORD of hosts** in Shiloh. And the two sons of Eli, Hophni and Phinehas, the priests of the LORD, were there.*

⁴And when the time was that Elkanah offered, he gave to Peninnah his wife, and to all her sons and her daughters, portions:

⁵But unto Hannah he gave a worthy portion; for he loved Hannah: but the LORD had shut up her womb.

⁶And her adversary also provoked her sore, for to make her fret, because the LORD had shut up her womb.

⁷And as he did so year by year, when she went up to the house of the LORD, so she provoked her; therefore she wept, and did not eat.

⁸Then said Elkanah her husband to her, Hannah, why weepest thou? and why eatest thou not? and why is thy heart grieved? am not I better to thee than ten sons?

⁹So Hannah rose up after they had eaten in Shiloh, and after they had drunk. Now Eli the priest sat upon a seat by a post of the temple of the LORD.

¹⁰And she was in bitterness of soul, and prayed unto the LORD, and wept sore.

*¹¹And **she vowed a vow,** and said, O LORD of hosts, **if thou wilt indeed look on the affliction of thine handmaid, and remember me, and not forget thine handmaid, but wilt give unto thine handmaid a man child, then I will give him unto the LORD all the days of his life, and there shall no razor come upon his head.***

¹²And it came to pass, as she continued praying before the LORD, that Eli marked her mouth.

*¹³Now Hannah, **she spake in her heart; only her lips moved, but her voice was not heard:** therefore Eli thought she had been drunken.*

¹⁴And Eli said unto her, How long wilt thou be drunken? put away thy wine from thee.

¹⁵And Hannah answered and said, No, my lord, **I am a woman of a sorrowful spirit: I have drunk neither wine nor strong drink, but have poured out my soul before the LORD.**

¹⁶Count not thine handmaid for a daughter of Belial: **for out of the abundance of my complaint and grief have I spoken hitherto.**

¹⁷Then Eli answered and said, Go in peace: and the God of Israel grant thee thy petition that thou hast asked of him.

*¹⁸***And she said, Let thine handmaid find grace in thy sight.** *So the woman went her way, and did eat,* **and her countenance was no more sad.**

Now that we have read the story, we are able to identify with Hannah and determine the reason for her prayers; how she prayed and what resulted from those prayers. The reason Hannah prayed was consistent with why most people pray today; and that is for the desire of their heart; among many other things. Hannah was a barren woman and wanted a man child as a means of eliminating the scorn and mockery associated with her barrenness.

I know quite a few barren women who are content to remain in that condition and yet be of service to the Lord. I would not agree, however, with anyone who proclaims barrenness to be a good thing because it was not meant to be that way in the genesis of time. In Genesis 1:26-28 says, *"And God said, Let us make man in our image, after our likeness: and let them have dominion over the fish of the sea, and over the fowl of the air, and over the cattle, and over all the earth, and over every creeping thing that creepeth upon the earth.*

²⁷So God created man in his own image, in the image of God created he him; male and female created he them.

²⁸And God blessed them, and God said unto them, Be fruitful, and multiply, and replenish the earth, and subdue it: and have dominion over the fish of the sea, and over the fowl of the air, and over every living thing that moveth upon the earth." So it was God's intention for women to be fruitful and multiply;

and that's the stand I take. But we are in an age where modern medicine and sophisticated medical techniques can literally put an end to the unfruitfulness of barrenness. With the use of artificial insemination, a woman can produce a child and not just one, but many at the same time.

Hannah wanted a man child and so she prayed to the Lord of hosts; she prayed to God the Father for the desire of her heart. She prayed a silent prayer though her lips were moving. Sometimes we find ourselves in certain situations that we have to pray silent prayers. There is no reason to believe that God does not hear silent prayers because he heard Hannah's prayer; and if he heard hers then he can certainly hear ours. Listen to what Jesus said in Matthew 6:5-8, *"And when thou prayest, thou shalt not be as the hypocrites are: for they love to pray standing in the synagogues and in the corners of the streets, that they may be seen of men. Verily I say unto you, They have their reward.*

⁶But thou, when thou prayest, enter into thy closet, and when thou hast shut thy door, pray to thy Father which is in secret; and thy Father which seeth in secret shall reward thee openly.

⁷But when ye pray, use not vain repetitions, as the heathen do: for they think that they shall be heard for their much speaking.

⁸Be not ye therefore like unto them: for your Father knoweth what things ye have need of, before ye ask him."

Hannah's prayer was simple and to the point. She knew what she wanted, and she also knew what she would do when she receive it. There are many people today who don't really know what they want in life; far more what they would do if they received it. They live from day to day without a plan; or without goals for the future. We must first know what we want before we could ask for what we want. It is also important that we do not ask amiss because those prayers are usually unanswered. James 4:2-3 says, *"Ye lust, and have not: ye kill, and desire to have, and cannot obtain: ye fight and war, yet ye have not, because ye ask not.*

³Ye ask, and receive not, because ye ask amiss, that ye may consume it upon your lusts."

When Hannah prayed, she not only asked for a man child, but she vowed to dedicate him to the Lord. So her prayer was twofold in nature; a prayer of desire and a prayer of dedication. Such a prayer is consistent with the will of God. How many of us have prayed for something that we would turn over to the Lord? Most of us pray for what we want and we keep what we receive.

The bible says that God heard her prayers and granted her the desire of her heart (1 Samuel 1:19-20). Perhaps God had planted that prayer in her heart because Samuel became the last judge to rule over Israel, and the first to occupy the prophetic office. Then there was Saul who was Israel's first king because the people wanted a king that they could see and identify with. He failed as a king and was replaced by David; a man after God's own heart. So the book of 1st Samuel covers the reign from Eli to Samuel, from Samuel to King Saul, and then from King Saul to King David.

The prayer of Hannah was one of those silent prayers that God turns his ear to hear. Already he had seen the afflictions which she endured as a result of her barrenness; then he heard her cries. There was also agreement in prayer which is a key to answered prayers. Jesus said in Matthew 18:19-20, *"Again I say unto you, That if two of you shall agree on earth as touching any thing that they shall ask, it shall be done for them of my Father which is in heaven.*

20For where two or three are gathered together in my name, there am I in the midst of them."

So when we pray, we should not be reluctant to have someone agree with us for our desires. And so I come in agreement with you, right now, and pray that the God of Israel who is God over all, grant you the desire of your heart; and that you would be blessed and be a blessing to all those around you.

I pray this in Jesus' name; Amen.

Notes

Notes

CHAPTER EIGHT

Hindrances to Prayer

Unforgiveness

Unbelief

Dishonoring your spouse

Turning away from God's word

Disobedience to God's Commandments

Unconfessed sins

UNFORGIVENESS

There are many hindrances to prayer and some of them may have their effect prolonged by your unwillingness to comply with the word of God. For example, if you choose to be unforgiving to others, your prayers will not be answered. Unforgiveness is a hindrance over which you have total control because just as forgiveness is a choice that you make; unforgiveness is also subject to your choosing.

Think of hindrances as obstacles between you and God with the sole purpose of preventing your prayers from reaching the Father. This is unlike Jesus Christ who is the only mediator between God men (1 Timothy 2:5) whose role is to intercede for us (Hebrews 7:25) with the primary purpose that we remain as one body in Christ. In John 17:20-21 he prayed to the Father saying, "Neither pray I for these alone, but for them also which shall believe on me through their word;

²¹That they all may be one; as thou, Father, art in me, and I in thee, that they also may be one in us: that the world may believe that thou hast sent me."

We must take unforgiveness very seriously because it is a hindrance when we come before God to seek our own forgiveness. In Mark 11:24-25 Jesus spoke to his disciples concerning unforgiveness and prayer. This is what he said, *"Therefore I say unto you, What things soever ye desire,* **when ye pray,** *believe that ye receive them, and ye shall have them.*

²⁵*And when ye stand praying,* **forgive, if ye have ought against any***: that your Father also which is in heaven may forgive you your trespasses."*

In Matthew 18:23-34, Jesus told the parable of the unmerciful servant who became victimized by his unwillingness to forgive. This story paints a clear picture of what happens when a person chooses to be unforgiving. The parable is listed here for convenience:

Matthew 18:23-34 (King James Version)

23"Therefore is the kingdom of heaven likened unto a certain king, which would take account of his servants.

24And when he had begun to reckon, one was brought unto him, which owed him ten thousand talents.

25But forasmuch as he had not to pay, his lord commanded him to be sold, and his wife, and children, and all that he had, and payment to be made.

*26**The servant therefore fell down, and worshipped him**, saying, Lord, have patience with me, and I will pay thee all.*

*27Then **the lord of that servant was moved with compassion, and loosed him, and forgave him the debt.***

*28**But the same servant went out, and found one of his fellowservants, which owed him** an hundred pence: and he laid hands on him, and took him by the throat, saying, Pay me that thou owest.*

29And his fellowservant fell down at his feet, and besought him, saying, Have patience with me, and I will pay thee all.

*30**And he would not: but went and cast him into prison, till he should pay the debt.***

31So when his fellowservants saw what was done, they were very sorry, and came and told unto their lord all that was done.

*32**Then his lord, after that he had called him, said unto him, O thou wicked servant, I forgave thee all that debt, because thou desiredst me:***

³³Shouldest not thou also have had compassion on thy fellowservant, even as I had pity on thee?

*³⁴And **his lord was wroth, and delivered him to the tormentors**, till he should pay all that was due unto him."*

(Life Lesson)

We must forgive those who trespass against us because we ourselves trespass against the Lord by doing the things we ought not to do; even by going to places we ought not to go; yet the Lord forgives us when we confess those sins before him. If we refuse to forgive those who offend us, our heavenly Father will not forgive us when we offend him.

In Matthew 5:23-24 he spoke on the need for reconciliation which involves forgiveness. He said, *"Therefore if thou bring thy gift to the altar, and there rememberest that thy brother hath ought against thee; ²⁴Leave there thy gift before the altar, and go thy way; first be reconciled to thy brother, and then come and offer thy gift."*

Unforgiveness is a sin because it mocks what Jesus has done on the cross for the sin of the world. Not only did he die for the sin of the world, but he also asked the Father to forgive them for what they have done to him (Luke 23:34). For this reason, we should obey what the bible says in Ephesians 4:32, *"And be ye kind one to another, tenderhearted, forgiving one another, even as God for Christ's sake hath forgiven you."* Again in Colossians 3:13, *"Forbearing one another, and forgiving one another, if any man have a quarrel against any: even as Christ forgave you, so also do ye."*

Unforgiveness is as having a dead corpse tied to your back which would eventually release all its toxins into your body, as the dead decays. It would not be long before the living and the dead become as one; infested with the same maggots that eat the flesh of dead men.

Unforgiveness must not be allowed to remain in your heart because you will become infected to the point where your relationship with the Father would seem dim and distant. Please forgive anyone who may offended you; and always remember to also forgive yourself. Next we will talk about dishonoring your spouse which can be another hindrance to our prayers.

Scripture References:

1 Timothy 2:5

Hebrews 7:25

John 17:20-21

Mark 11:24-25

Matthew 18:23-34

Matthew 5:23-24

Luke 23:34

Colossians 3:13

UNBELIEF

In the gospel of Mark Chapter 9 verses 14-27 tells the story of a man who after making a request of Jesus (the Son of God who is God the Son) to heal his demoniac son, openly admitted that he had a measure of unbelief. He knew that unbelief would have hindered the answer to his prayer request; so without hesitation, with tears in his eyes, he humbly requested help for his unbelief; believing that he would receive it. In that emergency situation, it took the confessing of his unbelief in order for him to receive enough faith to believe that his unbelief would be removed. Confession brings forgiveness and restoration. 1 John 1:9 says, *"If we confess our sins, he is faithful and just to forgive us of our sins and to cleanse us of all unrighteousness."*

The man demonstrated his unbelief when he used the word "if" along with his request. He said to Jesus, *"And ofttimes it hath cast him into the fire, and into the waters, to destroy him:* **but if thou canst do anything,** *have compassion on us, and help us."* (Mark 9:22). But Jesus, recognizing his lack of faith which must have developed as a result of the disciples' inability to cast out the demon, said to the man, *"If thou canst believe, all things are possible to him that believeth (verse 23).* That was when the father cried out, and said with tears, *"Lord, I believe; help thou mine unbelief"* (verse 24). Jesus cast out the devil, and the boy was made whole. I should also mention that the father of the boy must have contributed to his own failure to receive his prayer request; for he must have asked the disciples with the same attitude of unbelief.

There is a great lesson to be learned from this incident: When we come to God in prayer, we must always come believing. Hebrews 11:6 says, *"But without faith it is impossible to please him: for he that cometh to God must believe that he is, and that he is a rewarder of them that diligently seek him."* When Jesus confronted the disciple Thomas to prove to him the credibility of the resurrection, he said to him, *"Reach hither thy finger, and behold my hands; and reach hither thy hand, and thrust it into my side: **and be not faithless, but believing**"* (John 20:27). So this brings up the question; "What is faith?" The answer is found in Hebrews 11:1 which says, *"Now faith is the substance of things hoped for, the evidence of things not seen.*

²For by it the elders obtained a good report."

Unbelief would block our entry into the rest that God hath prepared for us. Hebrews 3:19 says *"So we see that they could not enter in because of unbelief."* Just as God rested from his work, he wants us to rest from our works and enter into his rest. Some disciples were desperately hoping to work the works of God without fully understanding what the work of God was all about. Even some of us today do not know what it means to work the work of God. But Jesus made it quite clear in John 6:29 when he said, *"This is the work of God, that ye believe on him whom he hath sent."* It is that simple because *"God so loved the world, that he gave his only begotten Son, that whosoever believeth in him should not perish, but have everlasting life. God sent not his Son into the world to condemn the world; but that the world through him might be saved"* (John 3:16-17).

Jesus has completed the work of salvation and he said it twice to the Father: once in prayer, as we read in John 17:4 which says, *"I have glorified thee on the earth: I have finished the work which thou gavest me to do."* And again, with his final breath as he hung on the cross; just before he died, with unprecedented exactitude with the choice of words, he shouted, *"It is finished"* (John 19:30).

Unbelief and prayer is the same as dynamite without a fuse; there can be no explosion. When we come to God and mix our prayers with unbelief, we are not only tying the hands of God, but we are also disrespecting his integrity and everything that he stands for. No one should expect to receive from God when unbelief is mingled with our prayers. Listen to what James 1:5-8 says, *"If any of you lack wisdom, let him ask of God, that giveth to all men liberally, and upbraideth not; and it shall be given him.*

⁶But let him ask in faith, nothing wavering. For he that wavereth is like a wave of the sea driven with the wind and tossed.

⁷For let not that man think that he shall receive any thing of the Lord.

⁸A double minded man is unstable in all his ways."

A person can say "I do not believe this or that;" and that is acceptable because the story might be untrue or unbelievable. But to have unbelief is to lack faith in what is believable: a good example is in the story we told earlier in the book of Mark, Chapter 9, verses 14-27. Mark has another good example of how we should approach God when we come to him in prayer. First of all, there should be no unbelief, but confidence and faith in God and in the power of prayer. Mark 11:24 says, *"Therefore I say unto you, What things soever ye desire, when ye pray, believe that ye receive them, and ye shall have them."*

I want to leave you with these two scriptures that will show the difference in the result between unbelief and faith. It might be a good idea to memorize these verses if you don't know them already.

Matthew 13:58 says, *"And he (Jesus) did not many mighty works there because of their unbelief."*
Romans 4:20 says, *"He (Abraham) staggered not at the promise of God through unbelief; but was strong in faith, giving glory to God;"*

Scripture references:

Mark 9:14-27

1 John 1:9

Hebrews 11:6

John 20:27

Hebrews 11:1

Hebrews 3:19

John 6:29

John 3:16-17

John 17:4

John 19:30

James 1:5-8

Mark 11:24

Matthew 13:58

Romans 4:20

Notes

DISHONORING YOUR SPOUSE

What man would dishonour the wife whom he loves? It is sad to say but there are some men who dishonour and disrespect their wives and put them to an open shame. Husbands who do not respect their wives and refuse to show them love as the weaker vessel will have the same measure of success in prayer as those who do not have love. The Apostle Paul gave us a good example of this unfruitfulness not only in prayer, but in one's existence as a human being. In 1 Corinthians 13:1-8 he said, *"Though I speak with the tongues of men and of angels, and have not charity, I am become as sounding brass, or a tinkling cymbal.*

²And though I have the gift of prophecy, and understand all mysteries, and all knowledge; and though I have all faith, so that I could remove mountains, and have not charity, I am nothing.

³And though I bestow all my goods to feed the poor, and though I give my body to be burned, and have not charity, it profiteth me nothing.

⁴Charity suffereth long, and is kind; charity envieth not; charity vaunteth not itself, is not puffed up,

⁵Doth not behave itself unseemly, seeketh not her own, is not easily provoked, thinketh no evil;

⁶Rejoiceth not in iniquity, but rejoiceth in the truth;

⁷Beareth all things, believeth all things, hopeth all things, endureth all things.

8Charity never faileth: but whether there be prophecies, they shall fail; whether there be tongues, they shall cease; whether there be knowledge, it shall vanish away."

In order for our prayers to be effective and produce results, we must first have consideration for others especially our wives who are joined together with us as joint heirs of the grace of life. This lack of consideration is as "Unforgiveness" which Jesus taught when he spoke on anger and reconciliation in Matthew 5:23-24. We have mentioned this scripture in a previous lesson, but for the sake of internalization on the part of the reader, I have chosen to list it again. Here it is again: *23 "Therefore if thou bring thy gift to the altar, and there rememberest that thy brother hath ought against thee;*

24Leave there thy gift before the altar, and go thy way; first be reconciled to thy brother, and then come and offer thy gift."

What about the wives, can their prayers be hindered? The answer is yes. Just as Paul urged husbands to love their wives, he sent the same message to the wives. Ephesians 5:22-24 says, *"Wives, submit yourselves unto your own husbands, as unto the Lord.*

23For the husband is the head of the wife, even as Christ is the head of the church: and he is the saviour of the body.

24Therefore as the church is subject unto Christ, so let the wives be to their own husbands in every thing."

The wife has just as important a role to play in the success of the marriage and in the development of an effective prayer life. Everything she does can directly affect their relationship either for the better or for the worse. This does not mean, however, that the husband can abandon his wife for any reason. He has to exercise good judgment, wisdom, love and understanding; and do whatever is necessary to resolve the situation. The Apostle Paul, in his address to those Corinthians who were married, made a statement that seemed almost revolutionary since it had to do with the 'saved' and the 'unsaved.' Consider this first then we'll look at what he said to the Corinthians who were married. 2 Corinthians 6:14-18 says, *"Be ye not unequally yoked together with unbelievers: for what fellowship hath righteousness with unrighteousness? and what communion hath light with darkness?*

[15]And what concord hath Christ with Belial? or what part hath he that believeth with an infidel?

[16]And what agreement hath the temple of God with idols? for ye are the temple of the living God; as God hath said, I will dwell in them, and walk in them; and I will be their God, and they shall be my people.

[17]Wherefore come out from among them, and be ye separate, saith the Lord, and touch not the unclean thing; and I will receive you.

[18]And will be a Father unto you, and ye shall be my sons and daughters, saith the Lord Almighty."

Now this is what he said to those who were involved in mixed marriages: 1 Corinthians 7:12-16; *"But to the rest speak I, not the Lord: If any brother hath a wife that believeth not, and she be pleased to dwell with him, let him not put her away.*

[13]And the woman which hath an husband that believeth not, and if he be pleased to dwell with her, let her not leave him.

[14]For the unbelieving husband is sanctified by the wife, and the unbelieving wife is sanctified by the husband: else were your children unclean; but now are they holy.

[15]But if the unbelieving depart, let him depart. A brother or a sister is not under bondage in such cases: but God hath called us to peace.

[16]For what knowest thou, O wife, whether thou shalt save thy husband? or how knowest thou, O man, whether thou shalt save thy wife?"

This approach to the marriage expresses the love and grace of God abiding with patience and longsuffering. But God is merciful and just, and he will resolve the situation according to his word. Sometimes they work out well and sometimes they don't. If a wife, whether saved or unsaved, knew the principles upon which a successful marriage is based, she could have victory. But some wives are totally unaware of their responsibilities in the home and as a result of their ignorance; they defy all the basic rules for a successful marriage; not to mention an effective prayer life. It is important for the wife to know these basic rules for a successful marriage:

1   **She has been given to him as a help meet (or assistance),** to assist him where necessary. Genesis 2:18 says, *"And the LORD God said, It is not good that the man should be alone; I will make him an help meet for him."*

2   **She must be submissive unto her own husband as unto the Lord;** (in the things that pertain to the Lord) Ephesians 5:22. I say "things that pertain to the Lord because it would not be wise for her to carry out an act that would be unpleasing to the Lord simply because her husband told her to do so. To do what is wrong is a sin; and not to do what is right is also a sin. 1 John 5:17 says, *"All unrighteousness is sin:"* Another translation say, *"All wrongdoing is sin."*

3   **She must love her husband and her children, if any.** Some younger women must be taught the proper way to love their husbands, and for this reason the Apostle Paul wrote to Titus giving him certain instructions for the church. Remember we spoke of the lack of consideration for the wife which can hinder the prayers of the husband; well it also goes for the wife. Titus 2:4 says, *"That they the aged women may teach the young women to be sober, to love their husbands, to love their children,*

    ⁵To be discreet, chaste, keepers at home, good, obedient to their own husbands, that the word of God be not blasphemed".

4   **She must reverence her husband.** She must respect him because he is the head of the wife (Ephesians 5:23). The love and respect must be mutual between husband and wife. Ephesians 5:33 also says, *"Nevertheless let every one of you in particular so love his wife even as himself; and the wife see that she reverence her husband."* If the husband does wrong, the wife must maintain her role as a wife and not stray from the principles that govern her role as a wife. 1 Peter 3:1-2 says, *"Likewise, ye wives, be in subjection to your own husbands;*

that, if any obey not the word, they also may without the word be won by the conversation of the wives;

²While they behold your chaste conversation coupled with fear."

6   **She must be a good homemaker.** In today's society, women are occupying the workplace just as men and do not have mush time for the home; but that does not mean she cannot be a good homemaker. There are certain responsibilities in the home that the wife is more capable of performing; and so she should take care of those things. This is not to say that the husband is exempt from those things. He can assist when needed. The world and its customs concerning wives have changed in many ways and therefore both husband and wife must adapt to those changes. 1 Timothy 5:14 says, *"I will therefore that the younger women marry, bear children, guide the house, give none occasion to the adversary to speak reproachfully."*

I have mentioned these five basic rules or points for the sake of the women and especially for the men who read this book. I do hope they will adhere to these basic rules, as they are necessary in preventing their prayers from being hindered. I am certain that the wife can add to these points; and the husband may also be capable of doing the same; but if they begin with these, the rest will fall into place. Remember that love is the principal thing in a successful marriage; and it is that love that gets the attention of the Lord when you pray.

Scripture References:

1 Corinthians 13:1-8

Matthew 5:23-24

Ephesians 5:22-24

2 Corinthians 6:14-18

1 Corinthians 7:12-16

Genesis 2:18

Ephesians 5:22

1 John 5:17

Titus 2:4

Ephesians 5:23

Ephesians 5:33

1 Peter 3:1-2

1 Timothy 5:14

Notes

TURNING AWAY FROM GOD'S WORD

The scripture you are about to read could not be more explicit when it says, "*He that turneth away his ear from hearing the law, even his prayer shall be abomination*" *(Proverbs 28:9)* God will not answer the prayers of those who jeopardize their commitment to him and his word by indulging in the smallest measure of sin. Psalms 66:18 says, "*If I regard iniquity in my heart, the Lord will not hear me.*" This may seem harsh, but the prayers of a person who does not have a love and appreciation for God's word is equivalent to the noise made by a sounding gong, a sounding brass, or a tinkling cymbal. Such prayers rise as far as one's head and fall back to his mouth.

It is no lie when the bible says in Proverbs 15:29, "*The Lord is far from the wicked; but he heareth the prayers of the righteous.*" James 5:16 says, "*The effectual, fervent prayer of a righteous man availeth much.*" To turn away from God's word is the same as turning away from his Son Jesus Christ; for the bible says in John 1:1, "*In the beginning was the Word, and the Word was with God, and the Word was God.* John 1:14 says, "*And the Word was made flesh and dwelt among us; (and we beheld his glory, the glory as of the only begotten of the Father,) full of grace and truth.*" The Prophet Isaiah said, '*All we like sheep have gone astray; we have turned, each one to his own way;*" (Isaiah 53:6)

Turning away from God's word is not the same as rejecting his Word. One can turn away after receiving the Word, as we learn in John 6:66 which says, "*From that time many of his disciples went back, and walked no more with him.*" But those who reject the Word also reject Jesus Christ such as those described in 1 Corinthians 2:14 which declares, *"But the natural man receiveth not the things of the Spirit of God: for they are foolishness unto him: neither can he know them, because they are spiritually discerned."* The prayer of the natural man or the unsaved man that God will hear, is the prayer for salvation. John 6:37 says, *"All that the Father giveth me shall come to me; and him that cometh to me I will in no wise cast out."* That man is not turning from God's word but to it. But Jesus warned everyone saying, *"He that rejecteth me, and receiveth not my words, hath one that judgeth him: the word that I have spoken, the same shall judge him in the last day."*

To turn away from God's word is a sin; and all sin have consequences which can dramatically reduce the efficacy of our prayers. If your prayers do not get God's attention, they will not be answered. Isaiah 59:2 says, *"But your iniquities have separated between you and your God, and your sins have hid his face from you, that he will not hear."*

I pray that you would not be ignorant of these things; for they can have a rippling effect even unto your children. The Lord hath said by the Prophet Hosea, *"My people are destroyed for lack of knowledge: because thou hast rejected knowledge, I will also reject thee, that thou shalt be no priest to me: seeing thou hast forgotten the law of thy God, I will also forget thy children"* (Hosea 4:6). My admonition to you is to remain in God's word and enable him to hear your prayers and be blessed.

Scripture References:

Proverbs 28:9

Psalms 66:18

Proverbs 15:29

James 5:16

John 1:1

John 1:14

1 Corinthians 2:14

John 6:37

Isaiah 59:2

Hosea 4:6

Notes

DISOBEDIENCE TO GOD'S COMMANDMENTS

Disobedience to the Commandments of God will surely hinder your prayers and cause you not to hear from God. Not to hear from God is in itself an unanswered prayer because we are always seeking to hear from him. When we do not hear from him, we do not get what we desire of him. Perhaps I should say it this way; when he doesn't hear us, we do not get the petitions that we ask of him.

Think of a father and the way he disciplines his children; he rewards them when they obey his instructions, and he denies them when they disobey them. It is the same with God the Father. The Apostle John puts it this way, *"And whatsoever we ask, we receive of him, because we keep his commandments, and do those things that are pleasing in his sight.*

²³And this is his commandment, That we should believe on the name of his Son Jesus Christ, and love one another, as he gave us commandment." (1 John 3:22-23). The first part of this commandment may be translated as **eternal life** because Jesus said in John 17:3 in his prayer to the Father; *"And this is life eternal, that they might know thee the only true God, and Jesus Christ, whom thou hast sent."* The Apostle John, in his gospel wrote, *"But these are written, that ye might believe that Jesus is the Christ, the Son of God; and that believing ye might have life through his name."*

The second part of the commandment was given after he had completed the last supper with his disciples. In John 13:34-35 he said to them, *"A new commandment I give unto you, That ye love one another; as I have loved you, that ye also love one another.*

[35]By this shall all men know that ye are my disciples, if ye have love one to another."

So if we disobey this commandment by allowing ourselves to doubt the power, the provision and the promises that are wrapped up in the name of Jesus Christ then we have shut the ears of God by our own will. We have barricaded the way that leads to the Father. Jesus said in John 14:1, *"Ye believe in God, believe also in me."* In John 14:6 he reassured his disciples saying, *"I am the way, the truth, and the life; no man cometh unto the Father, but by me."* Our asking has no way of getting to the one who does the giving.

If we reject the commandment to love one another as Christ loved us, we are, in fact, rejecting his love also; and therefore our prayers cannot be answered. In John 14:15-17 he made a promise to his disciples; he said, *"If you love me, keep my commandments. [16]And I will pray the Father, and he shall give you another Comforter, that he may abide with you for ever;*

[17]Even the Spirit of truth; whom the world cannot receive, because it seeth him not, neither knoweth him: but ye know him; for he dwelleth with you, and shall be in you." Notice, Jesus said that he would pray the Father. He did not want them to feel any uncertainty as to whether or not they would receive the Holy Spirit. There is no indication that they could not have pray for themselves because in the gospel of Luke, he urged them to ask the Father for the Holy Spirit. Luke 11:13 says, *"If ye then, being evil, know how to give good gifts unto your children: how much more shall your heavenly Father give the Holy Spirit to them that ask him?"*

When we disobey God's command, we are handing ourselves over to the power of sin; and if we do not confess that sin, we can once again become a slave to that sin. There is no way that God can hear your prayers except through a sincere confession of your sins. Romans 6:11-14 says, *"Likewise reckon ye also yourselves to be dead indeed unto sin, but alive unto God through Jesus Christ our Lord.*

[12]Let not sin therefore reign in your mortal body, that ye should obey it in the lusts thereof.

¹³Neither yield ye your members as instruments of unrighteousness unto sin: but yield yourselves unto God, as those that are alive from the dead, and your members as instruments of righteousness unto God.

¹⁴For sin shall not have dominion over you: for ye are not under the law, but under grace."

When sin shows up at your door, let him know that the person who once lived here is dead, and he will go away; but will return again in another disguise. What this means is explained so gracefully in the book of James. James 4:7-10 declares, *"Submit yourselves therefore to God. Resist the devil, and he will flee from you.*

⁸Draw nigh to God, and he will draw nigh to you. Cleanse your hands, ye sinners; and purify your hearts, ye double minded.

⁹Be afflicted, and mourn, and weep: let your laughter be turned to mourning, and your joy to heaviness.

¹⁰Humble yourselves in the sight of the Lord, and he shall lift you up."

We need to come before the Lord with a prayer of repentance and he will hear us. 2 Chronicles 7:14 says, *"If my people, which are called by my name, shall humble themselves, and pray, and seek my face, and turn from their wicked ways; then will I hear from heaven, and will forgive their sin, and will heal their land."*

There are many other commandments in the bible and they may be found in the book of Deuteronomy Chapter 28; but the one that supersedes them all is **that we should believe on the name of his Son Jesus Christ, and love one another, as he gave us commandment** (1 John 3:23). This is the same as looking into a mirror and seeing the words as spoken by Jesus in Mark 12:29-31. He said, *"The first of all the commandments is, Hear, O Israel; The Lord our God is one Lord:*

³⁰And thou shalt love the Lord thy God with all thy heart, and with all thy soul, and with all thy mind, and with all thy strength: this is the first commandment.

³¹And the second is like, namely this, Thou shalt love thy neighbour as thyself. There is none other commandment greater than these."

If we disobey any of these commandments and fall into sin, we must first confess our sins to God, for his faithful and just to forgive us our sins and to cleanse us from all unrighteousness (1 John 1:9). Then we can lift our holy hands and pray to the Father in the name of his Son Jesus Christ and he will hear us. The bible says in 1 John 5:14-15, *"And this is the confidence that we have in him, that, if we ask any thing according to his will, he heareth us:*

¹⁵And if we know that he hear us, whatsoever we ask, we know that we have the petitions that we desired of him."

When we disobey his word;

Our prayer cannot be heard,

But when we confess our sins,

That's when the process begins.

Bless the Lord.

Scripture References:

1 John 3:22-23

John 17:3

John 20:31

John 13:34-35

John 14:1

John 14:6

John 14:15-17

Luke 11:13

Romans 6:11-14

James 4:7-10

2 Chronicles 7:14

Deuteronomy Chapter 28

Mark 12:29-31

1 John 1:9

1 John 5:14-15

Notes

CHAPTER NINE

Praying all kind of prayers

Ephesians 6:18

PRAYER OF THANKSGIVING

In all things, we ought to give thanks to the Lord. King David, in his many Psalms, gave thanks to the Lord. In Psalms 118:1 he said, *"Give thanks unto the Lord; for he is good: because his mercy endureth forever."* Psalms 105:1 says, *"O give thanks unto the Lord; call upon his name: make known his deeds among the people."*

In this prayer, we want to give thanks to God for all that he has done for us.

(Prayer)

Father,

We come to you in the name of Jesus Christ of Nazareth, your only begotten Son whom you offered as a sacrifice for the sin of the world. The bible says in Isaiah 53:4-5, *"he hath borne our griefs, and carried our sorrows: yet we did esteem him stricken, smitten of God, and afflicted.*

⁵But he was wounded for our transgressions, he was bruised for our iniquities: the chastisement of our peace was upon him; and with his stripes we are healed."

Father, we thank you for the healing that comes through Jesus Christ but most of all, O Lord, we thank you for salvation. We thank you for your word that declares, *"Neither is there salvation in any other: for there is none other name under heaven given among men, whereby we must be saved."*

We thank you for loving us and giving us the Holy Spirit to be our guide and Comforter (John 16:13 and 14:16).

Thank you for the people you have placed in our lives to help us and encourage us in our Christian journey.

I thank you for my parents who have raised me in the way I ought to go; and have prayed for the blessings of God to be upon me.

O Lord, as I come boldly unto the throne of grace to seek mercy, I know I will find grace to help in time of need; but I just want to thank you for saving my soul.

I thank you for the use of the name of Jesus, in whose name I offer this prayer of thanksgiving.

Thank you, Lord

In Jesus' name;

Amen.

Scripture References:

Psalms 118:1

Psalms 105:1

Isaiah 53:4-5

John 16:13

John 14:16

PRAYER OF FORGIVENESS

Forgiveness is a choice that we make; and it is also a choice that God has made, in that, while we were yet sinners Christ died for us (Romans 5:8). While we are able to come to the Father and ask his forgiveness, we must also remember to forgive ourselves otherwise we may continue to carry the burden and the guilt of the offence. We must cast it upon Jesus because he cares for us (1 Peter 5:7).

Heavenly Father, though we have been given the authority to come boldly unto your throne (Hebrews 4:16), we choose to come humbly in your presence because we have sinned against you and have offended you through our disobedience.

And so we repent for the wrong we have done and ask your forgiveness. We know that you are loving and kind, and if we confess our sins, you are faithful and just to forgive us our sins and to cleanse us of all unrighteousness (1 John 1:9).

Restore unto us, O Lord, the joy of our salvation, and uphold us with thy free spirit (Psalms 51:12) that we may once again come boldly in your presence to worship and to praise you.

Heal us, O Lord that we may be healed; save us from the evil that tries to disrupt our thought patterns which are focused on you; for we would rather be obedient and not sin against you than to offer sacrifices through our prayers as we seek forgiveness.

Be merciful unto us, precious Lord and forgive us our sins.
We ask of you, in the name of Jesus.
Amen.

Scripture References:

Romans 5:8
1 Peter 5:7
Hebrews 4:16
1 John 1:9
Psalms 51:12

PRAYER FOR GOD'S SALVATION

In the book of Acts, Chapter 16, we learn that the Apostle Paul and his companion Silas were beaten and put into prison for casting out an evil spirit from a damsel who was possessed with a spirit of divination. But God work miraculously by shaking foundation of the prison with an earthquake, thus all the doors were opened, and everyone's bands were loosed.

When the jailer realized what had happened, he tried to kill himself because he thought that the prisoners had escaped; and he would rather have died by his own hand than by the hand of the king's men for being incompetent in his duties as a guard.

But the Apostle Paul stopped him at that very moment assuring him that they were all accounted for. The jailer, realizing that he now owed his life to Paul and Silas, called for a light, and sprang in, and came trembling, and fell down before them. He brought them out of the prison cell and asked the question that many people even scholars are still asking today. The question is simply this: "What must I do to be saved?" In unison, and perhaps with the sound of a heavenly chorus, they both said, "**Believe on the Lord Jesus Christ, and thou shalt be saved, and thy house.**" (Acts 16:31)

In Mark 5:41, the bible tells the story of how Jesus raised Jairus' daughter from the dead.
And even so will he raise us up from the dead when he comes again.

1 Thessalonians 4:16-17says, ".For the Lord himself shall descend from heaven with a shout, with the voice of the archangel, and with the trump of God: and the dead in Christ shall rise first:

[17]Then we which are alive and remain shall be caught up together with them in the clouds, to meet the Lord in the air: and so shall we ever be with the Lord."

But you must have faith in God and in Jesus Christ.
You must believe in order to receive.
If you're not a Christian and you feel the prompting in your heart, don't resist it;
It is the Holy Spirit.
The Bible says that no one can come unto Jesus unless it were given unto him of the Father. *(John 6:65)*

So I urge you to do the right thing;
Receive Jesus as Your Savior and Lord.
He died on the cross for your sins and rose again on the third day.
He's alive and well;
Seated at the right hand of God the Father with all power and might.
It was only by the shedding of his blood that Jesus was able to reconcile us to the Father and bring us into a relationship with him once again. It was only by the shedding of his blood that we could then be born again by the Holy Spirit.
Think of a woman who has gone through her monthly menstrual cycle. It is only after the blood has ceased to flow that she is able to give birth to a child. In a similar manner, it was only after the shedding of blood and the subsequent death of Jesus that we could become born again of the Spirit. It was through the shedding of Jesus' blood that we have the remission of sins. The bible says, *"And almost all things are by the law purged with blood; and without shedding of blood is no remission."*

My friend,
Who do you think saved a wretch like me?
Yes, It is Jesus;
And by a simple prayer you can receive him into your life, if you haven't done so already. When you say this prayer, you will receive a new life;
You will be Born-Again.

This simple prayer is so powerful, it can and will change your life for ever;

Prayer

Heavenly Father,
I come before you and ask you to forgive me of my sins.
I believe that Jesus died on the cross for my sins;
And rose again on the third day;
So with my mouth, I confess the Lord Jesus,
And I believe in my heart that God raised him from the dead;
So according to Romans 10:9 which is your promise to us who would believe;
I am saved. Hallelujah.
I thank you Lord, and I give you all the praise and all the glory for saving my soul from eternal damnation.
Amen.

PRAYER OF SUBMISSION TO GOD

Submission has always been a very difficult subject for us to deal with; for every time the word is mentioned we become very defensive. This defense is our way of saying, "we do not want to be submissive to anyone." Some wives become very annoyed when they are directed to scriptures that talk about submission. For example; Ephesians 5:22-23 which says, *"Wives, submit yourselves unto your own husbands, as unto the Lord.*

23For the husband is the head of the wife, even as Christ is the head of the church: and he is the saviour of the body." Or Colossians 3:18 which declares, *"Wives, submit yourselves unto your own husbands, as it is fit in the Lord."*

But the message goes beyond wives; it extends to children, and each other, to every ordinance, and to elders; but most importantly, we must submit to God.

Ephesians 6:1 says, *"Children, obey (submit to) your parents in the Lord: for this is right.*
Ephesians 5:21 says, *"Submitting yourselves one to another in the fear of God."*

1 Peter 2:13 says, *"Submit yourselves to every ordinance of man for the Lord's sake: whether it be to the king, as supreme;*

14Or unto governors, as unto them that are sent by him for the punishment of evildoers, and for the praise of them that do well."

1 Peter 5:5 says, *"Likewise, ye younger, submit yourselves unto the elder. Yea, all of you be subject one to another, and be clothed with humility: for God resisteth the proud, and giveth grace to the humble."*

James 4:7 says, *"Submit yourselves therefore to God. Resist the devil, and he will flee from you."*

Father, I come to you in the name of Jesus, and I humbly submit myself before you as a little child; for you love the children of the world. You have declared in your word; in Mark 10:14-15, "Suffer the little children to come unto me, and forbid them not: for of such is the kingdom of God.

[15]Verily I say unto you, Whosoever shall not receive the kingdom of God as a little child, he shall not enter therein."

Precious Lord, I humble myself under your mighty hand that you mat exhalt me in due time.
I submit myself to those who are under your leadership and pray for their successful stewardship.
I bow my knees before you, and confess that Jesus Christ is Lord to the glory of God the Father (Philippians 2:10-11). There is none like unto you for you are God Almighty; creator of heaven and earth.
You are omnipotent;
You are omniscient;
You are omnipresent.
You are my God.
You are from everlasting to everlasting; (Psalms 90:20)
You are the mighty God, the everlasting Father; (Isaiah 9:6)
You are the everlasting God, the Lord, the Creator; (Isaiah 40:28)
You are the living God, and an everlasting King, (Jeremiah 10:10)
You have loved me with an everlasting love; therefore with lovingkindness you have drawn me; (Jeremiah 31:3)

I thank you Lord for the gift of salvation which comes by Jesus Christ alone.
I submit my thoughts, my emotions, my will and all that I am into your hands.
Mould me and create in me the person you want me to be;
And make me a blessing that I may be a blessing to others.
I pray this prayer in Jesus' name.
Amen.

Scripture References

Ephesians 5:22-23
Colossians 3:18
Ephesians 6:1
Ephesians 5:21
1 Peter 2:13
1 Peter 5:5
James 4:7
Mark 10:14-15,
Philippians 2:10-11

PRAYER FOR GOD'S PEACE

Jesus made a statement about peace more than two thousand years ago, and it still baffles people today. This is what he said, *"Peace I leave with you, my peace I give unto you: not as the world giveth, give I unto you. Let not your heart be troubled, neither let it be afraid."* (John 14:27) The peace that Jesus spoke about is the peace spoken of in the Book of Galatians. This peace is one of the nine attributes of the fruit of the Spirit as indicated in Galatians 5:22-23; the others are; love, joy, **(peace)**, longsuffering, gentleness, goodness, faith, meekness and temperance. No one can fully understand the magnitude of this peace. The Apostle Paul described it as *"the peace of God which passeth all understanding."*

It should be noted that the peace of God and the peace that we try to have among ourselves are not the same; though one gives rise to the other. The peace of God will give rise to the peace that we have with each other because it is wrapped up in love. While the peace among men can be accomplished, in part, through good works, agreements, peace treaties and the like; peace with God can only come through Jesus Christ. Romans 5:1-2 says, *"Therefore being justified by faith, we have peace with God through our Lord Jesus Christ:*

²By whom also we have access by faith into this grace wherein we stand, and rejoice in hope of the glory of God." Jesus Christ is the Prince of peace and our hope of glory. Isaiah 9:6 described him saying; *"For unto us a child is born, unto us a son is given: and the government shall be upon his shoulder: and his name shall be called Wonderful, Counsellor, The mighty God, The everlasting Father, The Prince of Peace."*

The peace of God is synonymous with his heavenly kingdom. Romans 14:17 says, *"For the kingdom of God is not meat and drink; but righteousness, and peace, and joy in the Holy Ghost."*

Many people today are desperate for true peace, but are unwilling to accept the Prince of Peace as their Lord and Saviour. There is a peace that may appear to be genuine, but in the final analysis, it will not stand the test of time. There is a joy that may seem to have lasting effect, but suddenly it disappears and give way to sadness and depression as thoughts of troubled past emerges. This peace and this joy are not of the Lord and should not be compared with the peace and joy that comes from God.

People today desire true peace. In spite of all their prosperity, they are still unhappy and unfulfilled. The peace of God is beyond human understanding; and we are not required to understand it; just to accept it as a gift from God. It's a gift that will guard our hearts and minds in Christ Jesus (Philippians 4:7).

The bottom line is that Jesus Christ is our peace (Ephesians 2:14); and since he is God incarnate (John 1:1 and 14), he is the peace of God and we need this peace to live out our lives in harmony with God now and forever.

Prayer

Heavenly Father,

As we come seeking your peace, we pray for the peace of Jerusalem; that all the people would come to believe and know that your Son Jesus Christ who died on the cross for the sin of the world; and rose again from the dead is the true Messiah who will establish his kingdom on earth; and of his kingdom there shall be no end.

We pray for your peace upon on those who reach out to you, and as many as would call upon your name.

I pray, O Lord, that you would bless this reader, and let the peace of God that passeth all understanding guard his or her heart and mind in Christ Jesus our Lord.

Saturate their spirit with your peace, and let them feel the anointing of the Holy Spirit that they may be able to worship and praise you all the day long.

Empower them that they may put on charity which is the bond of perfectness; and allow the peace of God to rule in their hearts.

I ask this in Jesus' name. Amen.

Scripture References

John 14:27
Galatians 5:22-23
Romans 5:1-2
Phil 4:7
Isaiah 9:6
Romans 14:17
Ephesians 2:14
John 1:1; 14
Psalms 122:6

PRAYER TO OVERCOME FEAR

Some definitions portray fear as the opposite of faith; and that might well be true; but another definition is found in the book of 1ˢᵗ John, Chapter 4 and verse 18 which says, *"There is no fear in love; but perfect love casteth out fear: because fear hath torment. He that feareth is not made perfect in love."* So if one has perfect love, there is no fear; but if there is fear then perfect love does not exist. The two cannot exist at the same time; it is one or the other.

In all of this, let us remember that God is love (1 John 4:8), and it is He who makes us perfect in himself. If we suffer from fear then we need to seek the love of God in our lives and allow *that love to be shed abroad in our hearts by the Holy Spirit which is given to us."*(Romans 5:5)

Fear can be a valuable asset for everyone because it is the alarm system that warns of impending danger. But fear has another dimension to it for it can be translated as reverence for God. When the bible says "we are to fear the Lord," it does not mean that we are to be afraid of the Lord but to reverence him.

God does not want us to fear as in 'being afraid; else why would he say to Abraham, "Fear not" (Genesis 15:1); and to Isaac, (Genesis 26:24); and to Jacob (Isaiah 43:5); and even to his disciples (Luke 12:32)? King David understood the true meaning of '**fear not**' and he expressed it when he wrote the 23ʳᵈ Psalm. Psalms 23:4 says, *"Yea, though I walk through the valley of the shadow of death, I will fear no evil: for thou art with me; thy rod and thy staff they comfort me."* When you are in the valley of death and still have confidence in God that he will protect you and deliver you out of evil; that is a true demonstration of one who has faith and trust in God's word.

The Lord does not want us to have fear, and for that reason he tells us to fear not. When we become born again, our spirit is not one that is saturated with fear but with reverence for God. 2 Timothy 1:7 says, *"For God hath not given us the spirit of fear; but of power, and of love, and of a sound mind."* Before we were born again, we had a spirit of bondage to fear; but that has been dealt with when Jesus died on the cross and rose again from the dead. Romans 8:15 says, *"For ye have not received the spirit of bondage again to fear; but ye have received the Spirit of adoption, whereby we cry, Abba, Father."*

I can remember the times before I became *a son of God* (John 1:12), I was afraid of death; but when I was born again, the fear was removed. I realized to be born once is to die twice; first naturally then spiritually. But to be born twice, or to be born again, is to die once and that is the natural death. The bible says in Hebrews 9:27, *"And as it is appointed unto men once to die, but after this the judgment:"* The judgment for those who have not accepted Jesus Christ as Lord and Saviour of their lives will experience the second death which is total separation from God.

There are also those who fear that tomorrow would be worse than today; that they may have nothing to eat, or to wear; and out of that fear derives covetousness which leads to trespasses and other forms of evil. The writer of the book of Hebrews addressed that situation and warned the Hebrews with these words; *"Let your conversation be without covetousness; and be content with such things as ye have: for he hath said, I will never leave thee, nor forsake thee.*

⁶So that we may boldly say, The Lord is my helper, and I will not fear what man shall do unto me." (Hebrews 13:5-6)

People may come against you and accuse you falsely; they may even try to deprive you of the basic necessities, but the word of God says that you must not be afraid. Psalms 40:17 says, *"But I am poor and needy; yet the Lord thinketh upon me: thou art my help and my deliverer; make no tarrying, O my God."* God is good and he is there to help us through the rough times when we call upon him. Psalms 46:1 declares, *"God is our refuge and strength, a very present help in trouble."*

Prayer

Almighty God,

Creator of the heavens and the earth; the sun, the moon and the stars;
I bow my knees before you with the fear of the Lord.
I have trusted in your Son Jesus Christ as my Lord and Saviour;
And therefore I will not be afraid of circumstances that would threaten our relationship.
I believe that nothing can separate us from the love of God that is in Christ Jesus our Lord.

There are times, O Lord, when I sense the spirit of fear, but I know that you have not given me the spirit of fear; but of power, and of love, and of a sound mind.
I know now that what I feel is challenging what I believe in an effort to put me in bondage again.
Fill me, O Lord, with your Holy Spirit that I may discern the truth in every situation.
And to the person, who is reading this book, pour out a blessing upon him or her and empower them to minister unto others the truth about your Son Jesus Christ;
How he was crucified; nailed to a cross where he died. He was buried in a tomb and on the third day, he rose again from the dead. He then ascended up to heaven and is seated at the right hand of God Father.

We thank the Lord Jesus for the promise he made in Revelation 3:20-21 which says, *"20Behold, I stand at the door, and knock: if any man hear my voice, and open the door, I will come in to him, and will sup with him, and he with me.*

21 To him that overcometh will I grant to sit with me in my throne, even as I also overcame, and am set down with my Father in his throne."

We thank you, Lord, and we bless you for your mercy and your kindness;

All in the name of Jesus Christ;

Amen.

Scripture References

1 John 4:18
1 John 4:8
Romans 5:5
Luke 12:32
Genesis 15:1
Genesis 26:24
Isaiah 43:5
Psalms 23:4
2 Timothy 1:7
Romans 8:15
Hebrews 9:27
Hebrews 13:5-6
Psalms 40:17
Psalms 46:1
Revelation 3:20-21

PRAYER FOR WISDOM

Proverbs 4:7 says, "Wisdom is the principal thing; therefore get wisdom: and with all thy getting get understanding. As important as it is to get wisdom, it is also vital that we get understanding. One writer said, "Understand that you may be understood. No one cares how much you know until they know how much you care." So there must be that element of love in all things that we do; even when we seek wisdom.

There are two types of wisdom: True wisdom which comes from God and false wisdom which does not come from the Father above. James 1:17 says, *"Every good gift and every perfect gift is from above, and cometh down from the Father of lights, with whom is no variableness, neither shadow of turning."* James 3:14-17 goes further by saying, *"14But if ye have bitter envying and strife in your hearts, glory not, and lie not against the truth.*

15This wisdom descendeth not from above, but is earthly, sensual, devilish.

16For where envying and strife is, there is confusion and every evil work.

17But the wisdom that is from above is first pure, then peaceable, gentle, and easy to be intreated, full of mercy and good fruits, without partiality, and without hypocrisy."

We must never forget that the bible teaches us that the wisdom of this world is foolishness with God (1 Corinthians 3:19).

God wants us to have wisdom and for this reason the bible says in James 1:5-8, *"5If any of you lack wisdom, let him ask of God, that giveth to all men liberally, and upbraideth not; and it shall be given him.*

⁶But let him ask in faith, nothing wavering. For he that wavereth is like a wave of the sea driven with the wind and tossed.

⁷For let not that man think that he shall receive any thing of the Lord.

⁸A double minded man is unstable in all his ways."

We all would like to have wisdom, but some of us do not understand what wisdom really is. The standard definition of wisdom is **"the ability to make sensible decisions and judgments based on personal knowledge and experience."** The biblical definition of wisdom is found in Job 28:28 which says, ***"And unto man he said, Behold, the fear of the LORD, that is wisdom; and to depart from evil is understanding."***

Throughout the bible, wisdom and understanding are most often linked together because the one compliments the other. The Psalmist said in Psalms 111:10, *"¹⁰The fear of the LORD is the beginning of wisdom: a good understanding have all they that do his commandments: his praise endureth for ever."*

Prayer

Heavenly Father,

O wise God, who by wisdom made the heavens;

and stretched out the earth above the waters, and made the great lights;

the sun and the moon and the stars;

Who upholdeth all things by the word of his power;

We give you praise.
We come, O Lord, in faith, and in the name of your precious Son, Jesus Christ;

And we ask for wisdom, and at the same time, Precious Lord, give us understanding.

For your word declares that wisdom is the principal thing; therefore we must get wisdom. And in all our getting, we must also get understanding.

We seek therefore, O Lord, your face; and we reverence your name in all the earth.

As we open our hearts to you and to your word, we are indeed expressing our fear of the Lord which, as you have declared, is the beginning of wisdom. We acknowledge it and we receive this first installment of your wisdom which we will demonstrate in our conversations and in our deeds.

We thank you, and we bless you;
In Jesus' name;
Amen.

Scripture References

Proverbs 4:7
James 1:17
James 3:14-17
1st Corinthians 3:19
James 1:5-8
Job 28:28
Psalms 111:10

PRAYER AGAINST TRIALS AND TEMPTATION

Before we say the prayer, I would like to talk a little on the subject of temptation. In the prayer that Jesus gave to his disciples, there is a section that says, *"Lead us not into Temptation; but Deliver Us from Evil."*

When I read that phrase, I can't help but think of the times when I was just a young lad. I used to hang around with my friends, looking for something to do; or some mischief to get into. That was fun, but sometimes it wasn't very funny. I am sure many of you have stolen something before; even if it was just a cookie, you're still guilty. The temptation is always before you, and all you have to do is to succumb to it.

A few days ago, I was walking through the mall and I saw a young woman dressed in shorts and a T-shirt with the words at the back that said, "Lead me not into Temptation, I've been there before." This brings up a very interesting question. Why would we have to ask God "to lead us not into temptation?" Does this mean that God does lead us into temptation? One thing for sure is that God does not tempt us, the devil does.

James 1:13-15 says;

[13]Let no man say when he is tempted, I am tempted of God: for God cannot be tempted with evil, neither tempteth he any man:

[14]But every man is tempted, when he is drawn away of his own lust, and enticed.

[15]Then when lust hath conceived, it bringeth forth sin: and sin, when it is finished, bringeth forth death.

Romans 6:23 says, "*The wages of sin is death;*"

Let us take a look at the first temptation as recorded in the book of Genesis, Chapter 3 verses 1-7 and see if we can observe some of the tactics of the tempter. In the Garden of Eden, Adam and Eve were tempted by the devil.

The passage reads as follows:

¹Now the serpent was more subtil than any beast of the field which the LORD God had made. And he said unto the woman, Yea, hath God said, Ye shall not eat of every tree of the garden?

²And the woman said unto the serpent, We may eat of the fruit of the trees of the garden:

³But of the fruit of the tree which is in the midst of the garden, God hath said, Ye shall not eat of it, neither shall ye touch it, lest ye die.

⁴And the serpent said unto the woman, Ye shall not surely die:

⁵For God doth know that in the day ye eat thereof, then your eyes shall be opened, and ye shall be as gods, knowing good and evil.

⁶And when the woman saw that the tree was good for food, and that it was pleasant to the eyes, and a tree to be desired to make one wise, she took of the fruit thereof, and did eat, and gave also unto her husband with her; and he did eat.

⁷And the eyes of them both were opened, and they knew that they were naked; and they sewed fig leaves together, and made themselves aprons.

Notice how the temptation came;
It appealed to the senses, to the emotions.
It was good for food; "taste, appetite"
It was pleasing to the eye; "looked good"
It was good for wisdom; "they could become wise."
What they did wrong and sometimes we do the same; is to prolong the discourse with the tempter and fall prey to the temptations. In so doing, we rebel against God's will.

There is nothing wrong with temptation; for we will always be tempted. The temptation helps us to determine how strong or vulnerable we are in certain areas of our lives. James 1:2-4 says, *"My brethren, count it all joy when ye fall into divers temptations;*

3Knowing this, that the trying of your faith worketh patience.

4But let patience have her perfect work, that ye may be perfect and entire, wanting nothing."

But God is good, and he is always looking out **for** us, as long as we are looking out **to** him. James 4:8 says, *"Draw near to God and he will draw near to you."* God is watching to see how much you are able to bear; how much of the temptation you can resist. 1 Corinthians 10:13 says, *"There hath no temptation taken you but such as is common to man: but God is faithful, who will not suffer you to be tempted above that ye are able; but will with the temptation also make a way to escape, that ye may be able to bear it."*

The mind is the target for the temptation. The imagination is a centre in the mind that produces an image that will result in an action; and that's where the battle takes place.
For this reason the Bible says in 2 Corinthians 10:4-5; *(For the weapons of our warfare are not carnal, but mighty through God to the pulling down of strong holds;)*

5 Casting down imaginations, and every high thing that exalteth itself against the knowledge of God, and bringing into captivity every thought to the obedience of Christ;

Let's talk about strongholds, for a moment. What is a stronghold? A stronghold is a place in the mind where thoughts are kept, and fortified by other thoughts in order to justify your behavior; and keep you in addiction to a particular behavior or habit. For instance, you may be addicted to smoking cigarettes or other grassy weeds and you would not stop because you claim that it relaxes you, it keeps you calm; just to mention a few excuses.

Again you may be having sex outside of your marriage on the basis that your wife or husband refuses to have sex with you. There's an excuse for everything all of which have become strongholds in your life. You are held captive by your own imagination. But the Word of God is able to tear down those strongholds and set you free.

Isaiah 10:27 says, *"And it shall come to pass in that day, that his burden shall be taken away from off thy shoulder, and his yoke from off thy neck, and the yoke shall be destroyed because of the anointing."*

Acts 10:38 declares, *"How God anointed Jesus of Nazareth with the Holy Ghost and with power: who went about doing good and healing all that were oppressed of the devil; for God was with him."*

As for Adam and Eve;
They should have cast down their imaginations, and brought all those thoughts captive to the obedience of God. After all, God had told them what they could and could not do. But they gave in to the temptation and disobeyed God. It is sad to say, but there are always consequences for disobedience. Sometimes it could be death.
Matthew 26:41 says, *"Watch and pray, that ye enter not into temptation: the spirit indeed is willing, but the flesh is weak."*

Prayer

Father, we thank you for your promise that says, *"If we confess our sins, you are faithful and just to forgive us our sins and to cleanse us from all unrighteousness. (1 John 1:9)*
We know that sometimes we are weak but your strength is made perfect in weakness; and most assuredly, your grace is sufficient for us.

We thank you for your vigilance over our lives, and the trials and temptations that we face each day. We have the confidence in your word that says, "God is faithful, who will not suffer you to be tempted above that ye are able; but will with the temptation also make a way to escape, that ye may be able to bear it." (1 Corinthians 10:13)

Lord, we know that the battle is the Lord's and therefore we refuse to confront the enemy with our own strength lest we fail and become a victim instead of the victor. We stand therefore on your word and on the authority given us by the Lord Jesus Christ who said, "Behold, I give unto you power to tread on serpents and scorpions, and over all the power of the enemy: and nothing shall by any means hurt you." (Luke 10:19) And so, we come against every trial and temptation knowing that we will be victorious because of the name of Jesus.

Continue to watch over us, O Lord, as the good shepherd watches over the sheep. We pray that your Holy Spirit will continue to guide and protect us; as we yield to his authority in our lives.

Bless this reader and allow him or her to feel your presence as they open their heart to receive the blessing through your word.

I pray this prayer in Jesus' name

Amen.

Scripture References

James 1:13-15
Romans 6:23
Genesis 3:1-7
James 1:2-4
James 4:8
1 Corinthians 10:13
Luke 10:19
2 Corinthians 10:4-5
Isaiah 10:27
Acts 10:38
Matthew 26:41
1 John 1:9

PRAYER AGAINST BAD THOUGHTS

A thought is developed through the process of thinking and since we have the ability to think, we must hold ourselves responsible for both good and bad thoughts. There is also the imagination which is part of the thinking process and can be very detrimental if left unchecked. For this reason, the Apostle Paul was careful in ministering to the Philippians concerning this matter.

He persuaded them to be careful about the things they sought after; that they should bring their supplication before God with thanksgiving. Philippians 4:6-7 says, *"Be careful for nothing; but in every thing by prayer and supplication with thanksgiving let your requests be made known unto God.*

7And the peace of God, which passeth all understanding, shall keep your hearts and minds through Christ Jesus." And because he understood the frailty of the human heart; and *"how it is deceitful above all things"; (Jeremiah17:9)*, he urged them also to be careful about their thinking. In Philippians 4:8 he concluded by saying, *"Finally, brethren, whatsoever things are true, whatsoever things are honest, whatsoever things are just, whatsoever things are pure, whatsoever things are lovely, whatsoever things are of good report; if there be any virtue, and if there be any praise, think on these things."*

But what should someone do when he or she is inadvertently having bad thoughts? Is there a biblical principle to deal with such situations? Indeed, the bible is the final arbitration in all matters concerning our spiritual lives. Thoughts are spiritual and cannot be seen until they are manifested in a person's character. There is a course of action that takes place from a thought to the development of a person's character.

The only course of action for bad thoughts is to cast them down and the imaginations and every high thing that tries to exhalt itself against the knowledge of God, and bring into captivity every thought to the obedience of Christ. (2 Corinthians 10:4-5)

Thoughts give way to emotions which trigger decision making. When the decision is established, it produces an action which can easily form habits. The habits are the key factor in the development of the person's character which ultimately leads him to his destiny. This process works for both good and evil outcomes. Now it becomes clear why the Apostle Paul urged the Philippians to think on good things (Philippians 4:8).

There are other avenues that the devil uses to divert our attention from the Lord and unto ourselves because he knows that we are helpless when we are focused on ourselves. For example: When Jesus told Peter to get out of the ship and walk on the sea, he did as he was told; but as soon as he took his eyes away from Jesus and focused on the howling wind and the waves, he began to sink and shouted for help (Matthew 14:25-30). This is what happens when we begin to trust in our own ability. Proverbs 3:5-6 says, *"Trust in the LORD with all thine heart; and lean not unto thine own understanding.*

⁶In all thy ways acknowledge him, and he shall direct thy paths."

We must always be on our guard because the devil is constantly at work; trying to get us to relinquish our faith which we have in Jesus Christ. Peter addressed those believers in the Roman provinces of Asia Minor and warned them against persecution and tactics of the devil. 1 Peter 5:8-9 says, *"Be sober, be vigilant; because your adversary the devil, as a roaring lion, walketh about, seeking whom he may devour:*

⁹Whom resist stedfast in the faith, knowing that the same afflictions are accomplished in your brethren that are in the world."

The Apostle Paul also warned the Ephesians in this regard. In Ephesians 6:10-18, he taught them how to prepare themselves for battle against all the wiles of the devil; and that includes suggestive thoughts that seem to come from within. This is what he said:

[10] "Finally, my brethren, be strong in the Lord, and in the power of his might.

[11] Put on the whole armour of God, that ye may be able to stand against the wiles of the devil.

[12] For we wrestle not against flesh and blood, but against principalities, against powers, against the rulers of the darkness of this world, against spiritual wickedness in high places.

[13] Wherefore take unto you the whole armour of God, that ye may be able to withstand in the evil day, and having done all, to stand.

[14] Stand therefore, having your loins girt about with truth, and having on the breastplate of righteousness;

[15] And your feet shod with the preparation of the gospel of peace;

[16] Above all, taking the shield of faith, wherewith ye shall be able to quench all the fiery darts of the wicked.

[17] And take the helmet of salvation, and the sword of the Spirit, which is the word of God:

[18] Praying always with all prayer and supplication in the Spirit, and watching thereunto with all perseverance and supplication for all saints;"

We have to be very careful with the way we manage our thought patterns. We must be careful how we hear; and how we interpret things because our imagination is involved in our hearing. We need the grace of God to help us to analyze every thought that enters our mind, lest we be led astray by our own imagination.

Prayer

Heavenly Father, Lord God Almighty,
The omniscient God who knoweth the thoughts of man (Psalms 94:11);
We stand in your presence knowing that you are in full view and knowledge of our thoughts; even the very secret thoughts of our heart.

Therefore we surrender our minds to the leading of the Holy Spirit that he may lead us into those areas of your word where our minds can be renewed.

We seek, O Lord, to be renewed in the spirit of our mind;
Help us *not to be conformed to this world; but to be transformed by the renewing of our minds, that we may prove what is that good, and acceptable, and perfect will of God.* (Romans 12:2)

Lord you know what is in my heart; you know the bad thoughts that sometimes find their way in; even without my consent; and how I despise the thought.

Even as the Psalmist has said, I now say, "Search me, O God, and know my heart; try me, and know my thoughts;
And see if there be any wicked way in me, and lead me in the way everlasting. (Psalms 139:23-24)

Remove any thoughts that are not of you, O Lord and enable me to replace them with thoughts of your majestic kingdom and the glory that radiates from your Son Jesus Christ as he awaits the moment of his triumphant return to snatch away his bride, the church.

Take this mind of mine and help me to understand that ***I now have the mind of Christ*** (1 Corinthians 2:16) because he lives in me through the Holy Spirit.
I renounce the thoughts of evil and open my mind to receive the thoughts of Christ.
I pray this prayer, in Jesus' name.
Amen.

Scripture References

Philippians 4:6-8
Jeremiah 17:9
2nd Corinthians 10:4-5
Matthew 14:25-30
Proverbs 3:5-6

1 Peter 5:8-9
Ephesians 6:10-18
Psalms 94:11
Romans 12:2
Psalms 139:23-24
1 Corinthians 2:16

PRAYER TO BE SET FREE
FROM A TROUBLED PAST

I often ponder on the three dimensions of time; namely the present, the future and the past and have concluded that the present is now; the future is one step ahead; and the past is one step behind. The past is the present realized in its entirety; the future is the present yet to be realized. Though we can change the outcome of the future by adjusting the present; we cannot affect the past because it is long gone.

So the present is the key to both a good future and a past that is worth talking about. There are some of us who have had a miserable past; and though it is long gone, they continually enact those experiences; making the past a present reality.

There is a story in the bible about a man named Joseph who, after many trials and tribulations, even by the hands of his own brothers was able to gain the favor of the king of Egypt; and become the 'Prime Minister' of that country. His power and authority was over everyone in the land. Pharaoh, the king, said to him, "*Thou shalt be over my house, and according unto thy word shall all my people be ruled: only in the throne will I be greater than thou.*

41 And Pharaoh said to Joseph, "See, I have set you over all the land of Egypt."

42 Then Pharaoh took his signet ring off his hand and put it on Joseph's hand; and he clothed him in garments of fine linen and put a gold chain around his neck.

43 And he had him ride in the second chariot which he had; and they cried out before him, "Bow the knee!" So he set him over all the land of Egypt. (Genesis 41:40-43)

This is the same man who was sold as a slave by his own brothers. He was also falsely accused of rape, and put into prison. He had a past experiences that could have made his future amount to naught but he chose to live life with a positive attitude; not looking to the past but to the future. He trusted in God for a good future. Jeremiah 29:11 says, *"For I know the thoughts that I think toward you, says the LORD, thoughts of peace and not of evil, to give you a future and a hope."*

We need to look to the future and leave the past behind. Genesis 41:50-52 spoke of Joseph having two sons whom he called Manasseh and Ephraim because those names had a spiritual reflection on what God had done to him concerning his past and for him concerning his future.
The bible says, *And to Joseph were born two sons before the years of famine came, whom Asenath, the daughter of Poti-Pherah priest of On, bore to him.*

51 Joseph called the name of the firstborn Manasseh: "For God has made me forget all my toil and all my father's house."

52 And the name of the second he called Ephraim: "For God has caused me to be fruitful in the land of my affliction."

We need to put the past behind us and look forward to the future; and what God has in store for us. It is the only way we can expose the true potential of what lies deep down inside of us. The Apostle Paul said in Philippians 3:13-15, *"Brethren, I do not count myself to have apprehended; but one thing I do, forgetting those things which are behind and reaching forward to those things which are ahead,*

14 I press toward the goal for the prize of the upward call of God in Christ Jesus.

15 Therefore let us, as many as are mature, have this mind; and if in anything you think otherwise, God will reveal even this to you."

We must not live in the memories of a hurtful past because we are a new creation in Christ Jesus. 2 Corinthians 5:17 says, *"Therefore, if anyone is in Christ, he is a new creation; old things have passed away; behold, all things have become new."* Romans 6:3-4 says, *"Or do you not know that as many of us as were baptized into Christ Jesus were baptized into His death?* [4] *Therefore we were buried with Him through baptism into death, that just as Christ was raised from the dead by the glory of the Father, even so we also should walk in newness of life."*

We must not hold on to the past; we must let it go, and move on. We have to come to that place where we can be set free. That place is in the presence of the Lord. Cry out to the Lord to remove your past from your mind; cry out to him for your children to be set free. Ask the Lord to fill them with his Spirit that they may never hunger or thirst for the things of the world but for his righteousness. Lamentation 2:19 says, *"Arise, cry out in the night, at the beginning of the watches; Pour out your heart like water before the face of the Lord. Lift your hands toward Him for the life of your young children, who faint from hunger at the head of every street."*

Our heavenly Father has provided a way for us that we may never hunger or thirst again. In John 6:35, Jesus said, *"I am the bread of life. He who comes to Me shall never hunger, and he who believes in Me shall never thirst."* We can come to him with our troubling past and he will set us free and put us on the road to a brand new future. Jesus told a number of Jews who believed in him that *"if they continued in his word, then they would be his disciples; and they would know the truth, and the truth would make them free. If the Son therefore shall make you free, you shall be free indeed."* *(John 8:31-32 and 36)*

Prayer

Father,
I pray in the name of Jesus that anyone who reads this message that addresses a life that has been plagued with disappointments and hurts would come to realize that God is merciful and kind; and is a present held in time of trouble; that he is waiting with outstretched arms to receive them.

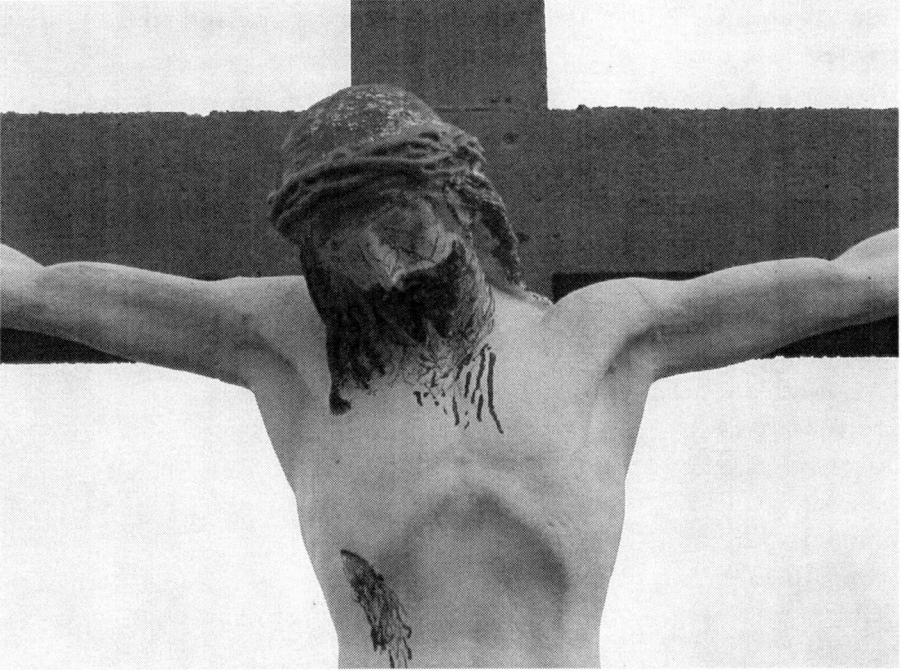

I pray that they would know and believe that God so loved the world that he gave his only begotten Son, Jesus Christ that whosoever believeth in him should not perish, but have everlasting life. For God did not send his Son into the world to condemn the world; but that the world through him might be saved (John 3:16-17)

I pray, O God that you would enable them, by your Spirit, to renew their minds by the Word of God. Set in their hearts a perpetual desire for the things of God and your word which is "*quick and powerful, and sharper than any twoedged sword, piercing even to the dividing asunder of soul and spirit, and of the joints and marrow, and is a discerner of the thoughts and intents of the heart.* (Hebrews 4:12)

Let the Light of this world who is Jesus (John 8:12), so shine in their hearts that they would have a clear passage along the way to a wonderful future that does not accommodate a hurtful or troubled past.
I thank you for your word which is "*a lamp unto my path (and unto their path also) and a light unto my path (and theirs also)."* (Psalms 119:105)

I ask this in Jesus' name; and I give him all the praise and all the glory as they testify to the power of his word.
Amen.

Scripture References:

Genesis 41:40-43
Genesis 41:50-52
Philippians 3:13-15
2nd Corinthians 5:17
Romans 6:3-4
Lamentation 2:19
John 6:35
John 8:31-32; 36
John 3:16-17
Hebrews 4:12
John 8:12
Psalms 119:105

PRAYER FOR YOUR NEED

It is important to know that God will satisfy our need but not our greed. There is a difference between what we want, and what we need. Some of the things that we want are sometimes not a necessity; but what we need are the essentials. We may want a Frigidaire when in fact; all we need is a cold drink. We may want a house, but all we really need is a bed to sleep on. It is vital that we get our priorities in order so that we can ascertain the difference between our wants and our needs.

Our needs do not always have to be material things; they can also be spiritual. We learn from the teachings of Jesus, in Matthew 6:33 that we should seek the kingdom of God and his righteousness, and all the things we need shall be added unto us.

According to the Apostle Paul, we must learn to be content with what we have; regardless of the situation that we are in. Philippians 4:11-13; 19, he said, *"for I have learned, in whatsoever state I am, therewith to be content.*

¹²I know both how to be abased, and I know how to abound: every where and in all things I am instructed both to be full and to be hungry, both to abound and to suffer need. ¹³I can do all things through Christ which strengtheneth me." He was confident when he said *"But my God shall supply all your need according to his riches in glory by Christ Jesus."* Indeed we must look to Jesus Christ for all our need because he has promised to be our provider. In John 6:35 he said, *"I am the bread of life: he that cometh to me shall never hunger; and he that believeth on me shall never thirst."*

One of the things that we always have the need of is the grace of God. We need the grace of God to help those who are in need. Without God's grace, we would not be saved; and without that grace we lack compassion and the desire to help others in need. We remain self centered and alienated from God. As individuals who have been purified by the blood of Jesus, *"we can come boldly unto the throne of grace to obtain mercy and find grace to help in time of need." (Hebrews 4:16).*

When God saved us and poured his spirit into us, *"his love is then shed abroad in our hearts by the Holy Spirit which is given unto us." (Romans 5:5)*

Therefore we must be content and let God be God in our lives. We must trust him and know that he will always provide for us. Psalms 37:25 says, *"I have been young, and now am old; yet have I not seen the righteous forsaken, nor his seed begging bread."*

Prayer

Heavenly Father,
We come to you in the name of Jesus that you may meet our need.
But before we ask of you, we want to magnify your name;
We want you to know that we cherish you and honour you as our heavenly Father.

We pray, Lord that your kingdom would come soon, and that your will be done on earth as it is in heaven. We ask that you will be established in our lives that we may please you now and forever.

Now we ask you, O Lord for our daily bread; for the things that we need to sustain our lives that we may be strong and ready to pursue the task that is set before us.

Protect us, O Heavenly Father from the evil one as we go forward to face another day.
We pray and we believe that you have heard us; and because we believe, we will receive.

We thank you, and we praise you for what you have done and what you are about to do;
In Jesus' name;
Amen.

Scripture References

Matthew 6:33
Philippians 4:11-13; 19
John 6:35
Hebrews 4:16
Romans 5:5
Psalms 37:25

THE LAST PRAYER IN THE BIBLE

Revelation 22:20

"Even so, come, Lord Jesus."

This prayer was the answer to what Jesus revealed to the Apostle John in the book of Revelation, Chapter 22, and verse 20. He promised saying, "*Surely I come quickly;*" to which John replied, *"Even so, come, Lord Jesus."*

This prayer was not an empty promise but the truth as revealed by Jesus Christ and is yet to come to pass. These last four words of promise hold the key to the redemption of all who believe in Jesus Christ and have trusted their lives into his hands. We believe that some day soon he will come in the clouds to snatch away all the true Christians who await his return. 2 Timothy 4:8 says, *"Henceforth there is laid up for me a crown of righteousness, which the Lord, the righteous judge, shall give me at that day: and not to me only, but unto all them also that love his appearing."*

We ought to be excited every moment of the way as we await that glorious day. Titus 2:13 says, *"Looking for that blessed hope, and the glorious appearing of the great God and our Saviour Jesus Christ;"*

1 Thessalonians 4:16-17 describes the moment saying, *"For the Lord himself shall descend from heaven with a shout, with the voice of the archangel, and with the trump of God: and the dead in Christ shall rise first:*

[17]Then we which are alive and remain shall be caught up together with them in the clouds, to meet the Lord in the air: and so shall we ever be with the Lord."

On that day, there will be no more unbelief to hinder our prayers because all our prayers would have been answered by his appearance.

We thank God the Father for the gift of his Son Jesus Christ. From that day onward, we shall always be with the Lord. *Wherefore (we shall) comfort one another with these words"* (1 Thessalonians 4:18).

Amen.

CONCLUSION

I would like to conclude this book with a prayer.

Father in heaven,

I thank you for all the inspiration you have given me through your Holy Spirit to be able to pen a portrait of your Son Jesus Christ whom you gave as a sacrifice for the sin of the world.

I pray, believing that the person who has read this book would be blessed by the truth that is revealed in scripture.

I pray not only for them, but all those who would come to believe in Jesus Christ through their word.

Precious Lord, anoint them with your anointing and fill them with the Holy Spirit that they may be empowered to do the work of the Kingdom of God.

I ask this in Jesus' name and I give him all the praise and all the glory. Amen.

Books Available

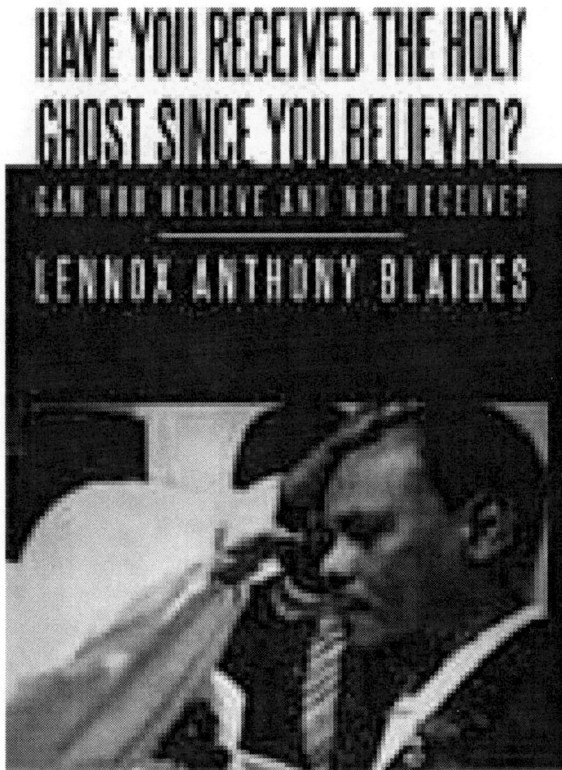

'Have you received the Holy Ghost since you believed' is a book written to challenge the spirituality of every believer; for not everyone that says 'I believe' is a true believer This subject has brought much debate in church circles, and though it is not an issue that should cause division, it has found its way on the top of the chart of debates; and has given way to factions even in the smallest of congregations.

In this book, I address this subject and other incidents of a similar nature that you may understand the significance of the question. You will be introduced to a man who believed all that the Apostles spoke but may not have received the Holy Ghost. I also speak of the baptism of John, the baptism of Jesus and the baptism of the Holy Spirit. Some Christians are still in doubt concerning the baptism by the Holy Spirit as spoken of in 1st Corinthians 12 verse 13.

When you read this book you will understand what the Apostle Paul was really asking the disciples when he posed the question to them in Acts 19 verse 2. I also give my testimony how the Lord saved me and my family from destruction; it will surely break your heart.

'Have you received the Holy Ghost since you believed' will take you to another step in your spiritual walk and cause you to examine the scriptures with greater depth and insight.

Available at:

Website: *www.authortree.com/thegateway2heaven*

Email: *thegateway2heaven@yahoo.com*

FROM THE
CRADLE
TO THE CROSS

FROM THE
GRAVE
TO THE SKY

LENNOX ANTHONY BLAIDES

FROM THE CRADLE TO THE CROSS

About the Book

'From the Cradle to the Cross' is about the life and death of the Lord Jesus Christ as he walked the earth two thousand years ago. There are four areas that make up the foundation for this book.

One: Prophecies concerning the birth of Jesus. Matthew gave a genealogy of Jesus to show his lineage to David, and that he was begotten by the Holy Ghost.

Two traces his footsteps from the river Jordan where he was baptized to Calvary where he would be crucified. Many prophecies were fulfilled, including his death.

This was not the end of Jesus' ministry because he would send another Comforter until he returns. John 14:16, Jesus said, "And I will pray the Father, and he shall give you another Comforter that he may abide with you for ever."

Three takes us into the grave where the 'tell-tale' signs of his return would be discovered. The witness in the grave would testify about his resurrection. We will discuss the significance of the empty tomb.

Four: The disciples witnessed Jesus departed to heaven. In this phase, Jesus speaks of brotherly love. He gave a new commandment that we should love one another as he loved us. He spoke to Peter about two aspects of Love; *'agapao* and *phileo.'* There is a reason for writing of this book.

The Apostle John wrote, "All these are written that ye might believe that Jesus is the Christ, the Son of God; and that believing ye might have life through his name."

Available at:

www.xlibris.com/FromtheCradletotheCross.html

Email: *thegateway2heaven@yahoo.com*

Lennox Anthony Blaides BCh.M, ACS

ABOUT THE AUTHOR

Teacher and Evangelist Lennox Anthony Blaides is a duly licensed minister in good standing with The Sure Foundation Fellowship, an ecclesiastical body with all the rights and privileges afforded by state laws and the U.S. Constitution to establish churches, perform weddings, funerals, baptisms and all ecclesiastical functions.

He has been preaching the Word of God for the past 16 years and has helped many people come to faith in Jesus Christ through the preaching of the Gospel of Jesus Christ. He has written several messages, which are available in audio and video formats.

Evangelist Blaides is the founder of: **The Gateway2Heaven,** a ministry that proclaims the Gospel of Jesus Christ to be the Power of God unto Salvation; and that there is no other name under heaven given among men, whereby we must be saved; and that name is Jesus Christ.

He is the author of:

'Have you received the Holy Ghost since you believed?'

'From the Cradle to the Cross'

'Pray One for Another.'

Email: thegateway2heaven@yahoo.com

Notes